Natural
Brilliance

Overcome any challenge...at will

Paul R. Scheele

Visit our Discussion Forum at
www.LearningStrategies.com

 **Learning Strategies Corporation**

Published by
Learning Strategies Corporation
2000 Plymouth Road
Minnetonka, Minnesota 55305-2335 USA
Toll-Free 1-888-800-2688 • 1-952-767-9800 • Fax 1-952-475-2373
Mail@LearningStrategies.com
www.LearningStrategies.com

Design by MartinRoss Design.

Library of Congress Catalog Number: 96-79312
ISBN-13: 978-0-925480-54-5

All photographs in this book are by PhotoReader and Natural Brilliance retreat participant Sonia Katchian of Photo Shuttle: Japan ©1996.

Contents

About Paul R. Scheele

Paul Scheele is the co-founder and creative program designer of Learning Strategies Corporation, a premier developer of self-improvement programs. Since 1981, Learning Strategies has been innovating leading-edge human development technologies that create ways for people to experience their potential. Paul has authored over fifty books and audio programs as well as over forty training programs taught in companies and schools around the world. He is an expert on learning how to learn and regularly addresses conferences and conventions.

His breakthrough developments include the PhotoReading whole mind system, a powerful system for processing written information at rates exceeding 25,000 words a minute. Hundreds of thousands of people have purchased his book *PhotoReading*.

Paul opened a way for individuals to make profound personal changes through an audio technology called Paraliminal learning. The audio program based on this book, *Natural Brilliance,* includes six Paraliminal learning sessions that help the listener automatically apply the Natural Brilliance model in daily life.

A unique combination of expertise in three powerful human development technologies—neuro-linguistic programming (NLP), whole mind learning, and preconscious processing—sets Paul apart from other authors. Paul has degrees in Biology and Learning and Human Development. His doctoral research in Leadership and Change has focused on Transformative Learning.

Learning Strategies Corporation, licensed by the Minnesota Higher Education Services Office of the Department of Education as a private school, publishes, licenses, and distributes Paul's work.

Preface

Since age nineteen as a second year student at the University of Minnesota, I have immersed myself in technologies of learning and human development with a single question in mind: How can people learn most effectively to use the tremendous resources within to create a high quality of life? My discoveries from over three decades of exploring this question have been captured in this book, distilled into the four-step Natural Brilliance model.

The Natural Brilliance model suggests a natural process we engage in when we learn effectively. As you read this book, you will quickly understand how to use it for your own success. You will learn about Natural Brilliance in Part 1, develop the skills in Part 2, and learn to apply the model throughout your life in Part 3. It is your choice to go as far as you wish to go. Take it all the way and you will overcome the blocks you face to accomplish the success you are determined to achieve.

The stories in this book and the events surrounding them are true. However, in most cases I have changed the names to provide anonymity. Let us know how you enjoy using the Natural Brilliance model so we can pass your experiences on to others who follow you.

Enjoy creating the high quality of life you desire.

Paul R. Scheele

Acknowledgments

Many thanks to those who have influenced the Natural Brilliance model: Bruce Overmier, Psychology of Learning professor; Dr. John Grinder, co-developer of NLP; Dr. Norman F. Dixon, friend and colleague, herald of the preconscious processor; Dr. Frank Smith, psycholinguist and reading maverick; Dr. Jerry Wellik, professor, colleague, and education rabble-rouser; Charles Parry and Linda Shrader, experiential learning specialists and collaborators in creating the Natural Brilliance model; Peter Kline, Integrative Learning expert; Patricia Danielson, accelerative learning expert and PhotoReading collaborator; Chris Sedcole, Direct Learning pioneer; Mark Kinnich, co-founder of Learning Strategies Corporation and paradoxical problem solver; Marcus Wynne, master training specialist; Mark Orth, psychologist and NLP pioneer; Rex Steven Sikes, NLP master trainer; Richard Bandler, co-developer of NLP and one of the creative geniuses of our age.

And I salute with admiration and appreciation my associates at Learning Strategies Corporation for without them you would not have this opportunity to experience your potential.

1

Reclaim Your Natural Brilliance

You have gone to a store, bought a book, and let it sit without ever reading it, right? Well, read this book and forever break the cycle of good intentions that fail. Think of times you have wanted to do something, knew that you could do it, but consistently failed to accomplish it. Let's not count them; let's figure out how to get what you want.

This is not procrastination we are talking about. I mean the situations where *part of you wants to proceed*, at the same time a part of you hesitates—wants to hold back—or find diversions. Giving my first speech at Toastmaster's International is a perfect example. Part of me wanted to do well, but a deeper part of me wanted to avoid the whole disastrous scene.

Toastmaster's Club #814 meets every Monday morning at the awful hour of 6:30 a.m. to develop public speaking skills. My assignment as a new member was to deliver an "icebreaker" speech introducing myself to 18 members attending the meeting. I spent the weekend scripting, typing, and perfecting my seven-minute speech. Since I had already developed skills as a seminar presenter, I was not worried about presenting a prepared speech.

I was the first of the three prepared speakers that November morning in 1978. As I walked to the lectern, my breathing was tense, and I felt a bit shaky arranging the notes in front of me. My nervousness did not subside as I got into my presentation. My voice sounded fast and high-pitched. My heart was beating fast, and soon I started feeling faint. I paused midway through a sentence to collect my wits and looked up at the audience. The room blurred and rocked slightly from side to side, and, when I glanced down, my notes receded rapidly from sight.

My strange long-drawn-out pause had several people giggling nervously, waiting for me to complete my sentence. No such luck. I felt if I did not sit down quickly, my knees would buckle.

"I-I've got to sit down," I stammered in apology. Pale, I stumbled back to my chair. I had no explanation for the questions, "What happened? Are you okay?" After the meeting, the club president's reassurance that I could give it a try next week did not help.

That week, a part of me pushed forward, "Yes, this is something I want to do. I want to get better at public speaking." At the same time, part of me wanted to get as far from Toastmasters as a car could drive, thinking "I can quit now. For Pete's sake, I almost passed out in the icebreaker speech! It can't get any worse...or can it?" To alleviate my failure, I used all my best mind control techniques; self-hypnosis, mind programming, visualization, and meditation.

Good news. There was no subconscious saboteur of my success. Bad news. The next week was no better. I stood up to deliver my speech again—same speech, same result. Only this time I had to run to the washroom within one minute of sitting down. Flu? I wish. Flu would have been a nice excuse, but, believe me, I could not blame any external cause for my apparent inability to accomplish my goal.

At the end of this second meeting I stood up, just before the president adjourned the group, to ask, "Would anyone be willing to stay afterward so I can finish this blasted icebreaker?" All but three members stayed, and I finished the speech with no problems.

John Seaton, the undisputed best Toastmaster in the club came up to me to say, "You know, Paul, I had the same experience in theological seminary when I had to deliver my first sermon. I just stood there gripping the pulpit and shaking all over. My professor said, 'John? Do you want to continue?' But I couldn't say a thing. I could only shake my head back and forth. 'John? Do you want to sit down?' I nodded my head up and down and stumbled back to my seat."

"It may sound weird, Paul," John continued, "but, after seven years of giving sermons, I still felt nervous when I gave my icebreaker here."

As he turned to leave, I realized John had given me a profound gift. All at once I witnessed that everyone in that room had given me the same gift. *It's okay to learn how to do this!* This book has a similar gift—a gift that all the best mind control techniques will never give you. You have profound inner resources now available to you, but unless you can gain access to them, they will remain locked away as great potential. In this book I shall show you how to find your Natural Brilliance and how to use it in any area of your life by taking four small steps.

Paradox: On the one hand, we possess amazing gifts as human beings. We are learning organisms, born into the world equipped to find answers to problems that face us. The human brain, mind, body, and emotions are designed to make us perfect learners, providing us with all we need for success in life. On the other hand, even with all our enormous capacities, many of us daily face the reality of not being able to accomplish important goals we have set for ourselves. Here we are holding apparently contradictory realities. Natural Brilliance explains why the contradiction exists and instantly bridges the gap between potential and accomplishment.

Natural Brilliance, a process unlike any single technique you may have used, is a four-step model for lifelong learning. It is a process for consistently breaking though to success in areas of your life where you are stuck. Like a riddle or a puzzle, the answer has been in your hands the whole time. Once you discover the answer, you may wonder how you could have missed it.

In this book you will find how to release your genius—your Natural Brilliance—using it to overcome barriers that have blocked you in the past to move you in the direction of your success.

Look Both Ways: Run Over by a One-Trial Learning

In Mount Vernon, New York, in 1960, I was five years old walking along Columbus Avenue. Suddenly I spied my oldest brother with his friend delivering newspapers across the street. Excited to see him, I called, "Lee! Lee!" waving my arms to get his attention. When he saw me and waved back, I dashed between two parked cars.

For years members of my family had coached me on the dangers of crossing streets, particularly of crossing busy Columbus Avenue. But in the next moment, the real learning behind all that coaching would be permanently set in place. A big black sedan slammed on its brakes but hit me with a horrible whack, sending me sprawling onto the road. The next tearful hours of being rushed to the hospital for x-rays and pokes by

doctors served to emphasize the message: Look both ways before you cross the street.

One-trial learning is something that remains a fascination to me. While studying the psychology of learning at college, I wondered, "When we learn something, really learn it, in a way we never forget it, what is involved?" If there is a natural and easy method to gain access to the inner learner, how does it work? Can we learn to solve problems and achieve success using such a method?

Years of inquiry pointed to a simple conclusion: YES! To discover the model for how to achieve such success in learning, watch babies. Infants and toddlers are naturally brilliant learners. Babies go for what interests them in the moment. They grab, see, hear, smell, feel, and taste it. They engage their full faculties, and everything in their experience instructs them how to proceed to ensure success. As adults you and I are the same magnificent creations, with bodies and brains that learn effectively.

Our ability to learn and influence our ongoing behavior serves at the same moment as our greatest *asset* and our greatest *curse*. Creatures of habit, we make life easy to survive and simple to manage by creating daily routines—almost like programming a robot. But, our power to learn and habituate behaviors can also trap us.

Imagine the curse of living with a robot programmed with faulty or erroneous information. Our potential to pick up bad habits can take us to destinations far from where we want to go. For example, learning to avoid sharp, dangerous objects helps us as children, until the dentist needs to work on our teeth. As a parent, I was so good at teaching my son Scott to beware of needles that he developed a phobia of them. Fortunately, a unique capacity comes installed in our design as humans. Unlike most other creatures of the animal kingdom, we are given a special grace to use our mind effectively. We have the power to step out of our robot selves, witness our habitual and instinctive behavior, overcome fears and phobias, and, with wisdom, influence our lives in positive ways.

Lyla typifies the difference between animals and humans. Lyla, my brother's dog, was blessed and cursed. A mix of Labrador and German shepherd gave her a field-champion nose. But, as a puppy, she got scared when Glen accidentally dropped a cooking pot close to her. Her phobia made her gun-shy and worthless in the field. On the first blast from a shotgun, Lyla dashed for cover and cowered until Glen retrieved her—not exactly what he had had in mind when he bought a retriever. Lyla herself can never overcome her fear.

Humans, with the capacities of higher-order thinking, can overcome limiting behaviors and fears. In this book, you can identify self-limiting patterns of behavior that keep you from your goals. With the Natural Brilliance model you can liberate yourself from those traps and realize the benefits inherent in your magnificent humanness—your brilliant future.

Release Genius and Overcome Oscillations

Review every instance in your life when you faced a challenge and overcame it successfully. If you and I took the time to study those events, we could create a model for effective experiential learning—a model of success you could activate to release your genius whenever you wanted to. This book concentrates years of that kind of study into a simple four-step Natural Brilliance model, which you can use to produce results you desire.

Releasing genius is half the story. When my colleagues and I at Learning Strategies Corporation studied how people fail, we discovered a consistent pattern that invariably produced stuck states—an inability to learn or make progress. Think of problems you have been unable to solve in your personal or professional life. You will find contradictory forces. Part of you wants to push forward and succeed while another part wants to pull back and not risk failing. True? The physical, mental, and emotional systems oscillate with a push and pull that ends up freezing your potential for achievement. Natural Brilliance resolves these problems that you have never before consistently been able to conquer.

Imagine yourself born into the world, actively responding, interacting with everyone and everything to meet your needs. Every time you receive a strong negative reinforcer, it is as if a stop sign is erected right there in your experience of your world. Thereafter, your mind, body, and emotions will register "Stop!" every time you approach a similar situation. The more stop signs you obey in any given area of your life's experiences, the less willingness, courage, and creativity you will exhibit as time goes on.

Let us say that twenty to thirty years later you want to accomplish results in a particular area of your life—relationships, physical health, finances, learning—but every time you try to progress, you pull back internally. The result is that you oscillate between push and pull and never break through.

Oscillations produce stuck states—stagnant areas of our lives. Oscillation and stuck states prevent us from accessing our natural genius. The good news is that you can win your Natural Brilliance back and achieve the results you desire.

Change the Way You Change: No More Stuck States

The Natural Brilliance model has grown out of my years of work in the field of human development. Examining what works and what does not work to help a person change allowed me to notice a pattern. You may reach the same conclusion by drawing a quadrant model.

On the x-axis put "present situation" and "future situation." On the y-axis put "positive experiences" and "negative experiences."

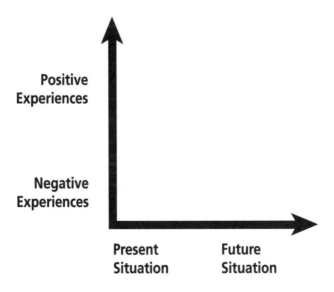

When you form a grid using these axes, you see a clear directive for approaching personal and professional change. It makes sense that anyone having negative experiences would move away from them toward achieving future positive experiences. Moving away from negative experiences toward achieving positive experiences is the basis for almost all the most positive mind development and personal success strategies. Billions of dollars of advice has been sold to people wanting to make their lives better by this simple model:

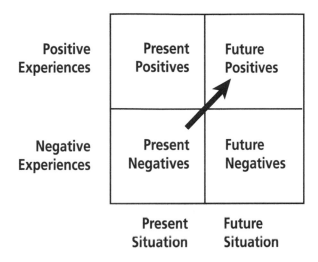

Unfortunately, such a one-dimensional process of change leaves two enormous gaps. Firstly, you risk *losing present positives* that are contained in the way you are living your life today. No matter how bad things are, there is "secondary gain," or some payoff, to the present situation. Secondly, one-dimensional change does not take into account the potential of *creating future negatives*. In other words, the grass is not necessarily all green on the other side of the fence.

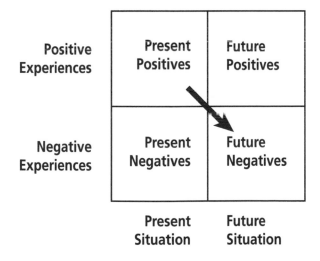

A model for human development must take into account all four quadrants of the grid. If not, the enormous negative consequences of losing present positives and creating future negatives will throw the unwitting personal achievement aspirant into an oscillation.

Perhaps you have attended a daylong "success seminar" where charismatic speakers whip you into a positive-thinking frenzy. Why is it that the effect lasts only three days? Because the pressures of the unattended two quadrants exert themselves consciously and unconsciously, forcing you to shift back into your accustomed stuck state. Even the Declaration of Independence spoke of this. "...and, accordingly, all experience hath shewn, that mankind are more disposed to suffer, while evils are sufferable, than to right themselves by abolishing the forms to which they are accustomed."

To break the endless oscillation and stagnation in stuck states, a model for human development and change must account for all four quadrants. You must keep the present positives while eliminating the present negatives. Simultaneously, you must maximize the future positives and minimize future negatives. Natural Brilliance does this and more.

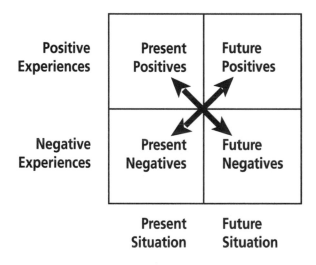

Applications of the Natural Brilliance model help you grow in areas of your life where you have never succeeded before. Using the exciting processes in Part 3 of this book, you can remove the stop signs that have kept you stuck and infuse your body and mind with new choices and pathways to success.

Here is an overview of the Natural Brilliance model so you can successfully make the changes you want in life.

Discover the Four-Step Natural Brilliance Model

Consciously using the four-step Natural Brilliance model provides a way out of stuck states by implementing the natural learning model the body-mind uses to accomplish success in learning. Now, whenever you feel yourself entering a stuck state, you can reverse the normal course of things to move away from failure toward success.

To say that you can solve any problem facing you is a bold claim. Since the early 1980s, I have focused my work on creative problem-solving, higher-order thinking, and resolving paradoxical problems. During these years I have created a model to articulate how successful individuals learn. I am excited to share this four-step model with you now.

Very simply, the steps are Release, Notice, Respond, Witness. I will expand the brief description of each step in Chapters 4 through 8.

Release

The first step, Release, drains stress out of the physical systems. Relaxing your body and mind is the essential first step to promote the optimal state for learning—relaxed alertness.

Tension and resistance characterize a person trying to change the present situation. Often, the person strains to avoid making the situation worse. Paradoxically, almost everything people instinctively do to remedy a bad situation makes it worse. Paradoxically, the best solution may also be counterintuitive, that is, against what they initially think will work.

If you ever learned to drive a car with manual transmission, you may remember how tense you felt. Think of your initial response when you realized you had to stop at a red light, on a hill, with cars pulling up behind you. Tension in your legs and arms. Panic growing in the pit of your stomach. Attempting to control everything perfectly. All these made it next to impossible to succeed. I remember one fellow who switched on the emergency flashers, pulled on the parking brake, and abandoned his pickup truck. He *knew* he was not going to succeed.

Tension and stress causes us to narrowly focus our attention. We manage micro details and miss the big picture. It is almost impossible to witness our own paradoxical responses. We are too close to the problem and too immersed in the oscillating system. Breakthrough happens when we make the connection that our attempts to keep everything in control are antithetical to relaxing enough to be in control.

You can release in many ways. Changing posture, eye-focus, breathing, and thoughts can produce a calming effect. By draining stress out of the body and mind, you automatically dampen or minimize the oscillation that keeps you in your stuck state. Simultaneously you restore your natural sensing acuity.

The human sensory systems are capable of perceiving minute changes in the world around and within. Tension blocks this capability. Release: pull your forehead off the tree long enough to see that you are in the forest, and immediately options will appear. When you put your sensory systems back online, the second step of the model is possible. Step out of tunnel vision, and the world opens up.

Notice

Notice means entering a state of increased awareness and paying attention to information in the present situation. When you attend to the input in your sensory systems, you will naturally generate creative options and promising responses.

Helen Keller's life story describes the primal life urge of the human organism—to make sense of its world. The human brain is a pattern-making device. It does everything it can to code and organize incoming sensory perceptions. Information processing is its job. Despite Helen's sensory limitations, she had a profound urge to make sense of her world.

When young Helen finally understood what her teacher Annie Sullivan had been trying to teach her, everything in her life changed. If you have ever seen *The Helen Keller Story,* with Patty Duke portraying young Helen, you know what a heart-wrenching moment it is when she makes the connection between actions and meanings.

"W-A-T-E-R." The sign language in her hand, the feeling of the water flowing from the pump, the shape of the word in her mouth all connected. Then, the rest of Helen's world cascaded together, and patterns began forming a cohesive whole.

The speed of the mind is tremendous. The inner mind works at making associations much faster than the conscious mind can duplicate. When given the proper direction, the whole mind can accomplish virtually any problem-solving task.

The step of Noticing involves becoming aware of what is happening around and in you. We have five physical senses to perceive our outside world. Corresponding to each is a similar sensory system represented in the mind. External sensory perceptions include all the information coming into the five physical sensory systems. Internal perceptions include inner pictures, imaginings, memories, emotional feelings, remembered tactile sensations, internal dialogue, voices and other sounds, even remembered smells and tastes.

From the rich information about your outer experience and inner experience, you can make decisions and respond to people and events. You can also develop a new point of view, a perceptual position other than being stuck. You can see what you are doing in the situation in which you are doing it.

The advantage of an "outside yourself" awareness is it opens the possibility for balance. Think of a teeter-totter or a seesaw on the school playground when you were a kid. Imagine trying to balance the thing by running on the top of it from one end to the other. Now, hop off it and choose a new position to work from—alongside the oscillating system. This time use your hands to dampen the oscillation and bring the teeter-totter into balance.

By combining the first two steps, Release and Notice, you achieve the optimal learning state, the state of relaxed alertness. Once you have developed relaxed alertness and increased your foundation of information, you can choose new responses from a rich set of options.

Respond

Any response either increases the oscillation and the inability to move, or it dampens the oscillation

and increases movement toward a satisfying outcome. Step 3 involves creating a response in order to discover how things change, for better or worse.

Anything you do has an effect, according to Newton's laws of physics. The objective of doing something, anything, is to pull yourself out of your stuck state so you can witness the effects of your new actions, whether positive or negative.

As children learn to walk, everything they do plays into their success. I used to love watching my boys when they were toddlers. I remember the first time Ben stood next to the couch triumphantly balancing on his pudgy little feet without holding on, his proud smile and gleaming eyes unmistakable testimony of the joy of learning. He took to bouncing up and down like a gymnast doing aerobic knee bends. Too much bounce and he would lose his grip and fall. No problem. Up again for another round.

Then one day he had coordinated muscles and balance enough to solo. On crazy legs he dashed across the carpeted floor in something that looked more like a controlled fall than walking. Intently he developed stopping, starting, and balancing without aid. Falling was perfectly important feedback, not failure but another step in the learning process.

The importance of the third step, Respond, is to take action. These actions will either make the situation better or not. In either case, movement within a system provides real and immediate feedback.

Once your brain recognizes your doing (or not doing) something makes your situation better or worse, you have the beginnings of change and the first step in gaining control of the outcomes you want to produce. When you feel you can cause your life to get better, you can generate a positive effect that builds self-confidence and self-esteem. Witnessing the results of your actions—Step 4 of the model—puts you in charge of producing the success you want.

Witness

In Step 4 you find a nonjudgmental position from which you observe learning taking place. Whether your response in Step 3 has succeeded or failed is not significant. The important thing is to get feedback that can lead to learning.

In this step the feeling is one of safety and blessing. Emotional safety and a sense of blessing were the essential components of my Toastmaster's experience. You will experience them as important evidence that you have made a breakthrough.

Think how babies learn to speak their native language. They have high intrinsic motivation to learn. They initiate their own learning, surrounded by highly visible models. Unlimited repetitions are okay, and everything they do produces an outcome, not a failure. For their efforts they get generous support, well-spaced rewards, and immediate feedback. Everything they learn is relevant. They never question whether they will succeed; they expect success.

Do you desire to break through to a new level of performance? The Natural Brilliance model leads you to replicate and reclaim the safety and blessings of your natural learning genius.

Consider that no task of learning is more complex than learning a language. Do you realize, you acquired many of your language skills long before you entered school? Unfortunately, many students think of school as a place of wounding. Natural Brilliance will assist you in overcoming your wounds and replacing them with the strengths of safety and blessing.

When they are learning to speak, babies automatically acknowledge their own authority. Their self-esteem grows as they learn. The great opportunity for you as an adult is to witness your continued learning each day. As you develop the Natural Brilliance in you, the results you create will light up your life.

Benefit from Natural Brilliance and Go Beyond

The four steps of Natural Brilliance—Release, Notice, Respond, Witness—are all skills you have already developed to a certain degree. This book will show you how to activate your Natural Brilliance to enjoy benefits immediately.

Let your Natural Brilliance shine throughout all areas of your life. You can overcome the oscillations and stuck states that have held you back where you have wanted to succeed. In the next chapter you can make long strides toward releasing your genius. I shall introduce the concepts of stuck states operating in your life and explain five principles that make Natural Brilliance an effective model for your own development.

Part 2 of this book will teach you all the components of the Natural Brilliance model, including the four steps and three attitudes essential to your moving effectively through the model. The chapters are written in a way to actually use specific abilities immediately and help you achieve desired results.

Part 3 offers potent new techniques, step-by-step processes that will blow out useless stuck states, resolve paradoxical problems that have kept you from achieving your personal and professional goals, and activate your genius. You will develop the skills of Direct Learning, Creative Problem-Solving, and the New Option Generator to boldly create the life you desire.

Activate Your Genius with Direct Learning

Direct Learning allows you to take authoritative written materials and blast new skills directly into your neurophysiology at 25,000 words a minute. Think how wonderful it would be to download the world's best ideas into your internal database. With PhotoReading you route valuable information into your inner mind. Then using the Direct Learning technique, you activate powerful new behaviors directly into your ongoing performance to achieve new results you desire. Direct Learning stands at the pinnacle of human development technologies because of the immense value it can provide you with ease and comfort.

When you realize your inner mind is your ally in personal and professional development, you can begin using it to make great strides in the direction of your goals. The fun of Direct Learning is that personal growth happens almost effortlessly.

Solve the Real Problem

Chapter 11: *Approach Paradoxical Problems with Creative Problem-Solving* introduces an important process for understanding and resolving paradoxical problems. It shows you how to define personal problems to ensure you generate solutions that work. It discloses the secrets of resolving problems that never seem to get better—no matter what you have done in the past.

Have you ever worked hard to resolve a problem only to discover that the problem comes back a week or two later? Crash diet programs are a classic example of immense effort followed by the returning problem. Often times, the loss of ten pounds is followed by a gain of 12 or 15 pounds. Some problems keep us on an endless roller coaster ride. Year after year, the same problem comes back—often with a vengeance.

Knowing how to define and approach such problems will make it possible to finally reach a destination of long-lasting success. Creative Problem-Solving will show you how.

Generate New Options

The New Option Generator, presented in Chapter 12, comes to you after fifteen years of development. It will probably be the most significant technique for breakthrough you will ever use. The process involves seven exercises that lead you step-by-step from stuck state to excellence.

The New Option Generator integrates the knowledge and skills you learn from the entire book. It extends the Natural Brilliance model by giving you physical evidence of the changes that occur as you release oscillation, notice new choices, respond with commitment to desired goals, and witness the outcomes you produce. Doing the exercises of this process will pull out the stop signs that may have prevented you from achieving success, revealing the potential you were born to express.

Summary

Do you already have a sense of how this book will help you discover your Natural Brilliance? This first chapter has introduced you to the techniques that will assist you in applying this model. Natural Brilliance is an approach to lifelong learning that can be applied in stages. Familiarize yourself with the model and its benefits by reading Part 1: *Orient to Your Natural Brilliance*. To learn the component skills of Natural Brilliance and discover the benefits in your everyday life, read Part 2: *Gain the Skills of Natural Brilliance* and practice the suggested exercises. To enrich your use of Natural Brilliance and gain maximum benefit, read Part 3: *Apply Natural Brilliance*.

What do you want to receive from your interaction with Natural Brilliance? Feel free to clarify your purpose and approach the book in the way that works best for you. Above all, enjoy!

> **Life is made of millions of moments, but we live only one of these moments at a time. As we begin to change this moment, we begin to change our lives.**
>
> **D. Trinidad Hunt**
> ***Remember to Remember Who You Are***

2

Understand Your Stuck States

You know you need to change your life when you are not where you want to be. If your present state does not match your desired outcome, then set a goal by asking yourself, "What do I want?" After specifying a desired result, you achieve your goal by filling in the gap between where you are now and where you want to be. Using the four steps of Natural Brilliance, you can create an elegant path for achieving whatever you want.

When your thoughts, feelings, and actions are filled with the purpose of living your desired new life, you magnetize yourself, attracting to you all you need. It is surprising and delightful the way resources come rushing into your life to fill the gap. Life can be wonderful and easy, but sometimes—in spite of your best efforts—your journey may feel like one huge stop sign. You know what you want, but you cannot seem to make the results show up.

In this chapter you will understand why stuck states exist, how they multiply, which benefits keep them in place, and what opportunities you have to move beyond them. In Part 2 you discover how to achieve goals when everything you have already tried has not worked. You will find out what you can do when you are stuck to activate your genius.

Analyze Stuck States and Take the First Step Out

Brian entered the ballroom through the back doors. "Stay right there!" I said to him through my microphone. The 250 company managers turned to look at him from their seats. I explained, "The group has determined one simple task for you to perform in this room. Your job is to figure out what it is and do it. The only information you will receive is my ringing this bell EVERY TIME you do something *wrong*."

After he had volunteered to take part in an exercise and left the room, the group had decided to have him walk up to the flip chart and turn the page.

Brian walked into the room toward the front. He turned to the left and the bell rang out "WRONG!" He stopped. With hesitation, Brian walked forward toward the flip chart. Everyone silently watched as he turned away from the flip chart toward the podium. The bell stopped him in his tracks. He looked about without moving his feet, tentatively turned around, and headed for the flip chart. No bell. When he walked passed it toward the overhead projector, he got a bell again which halted him in front of the flip chart. Now, more cautiously than ever, he picked up a red marker; "RING!" then, quickly  put it down. He tried a black marker; "RING!" After the same response with the blue and green markers, Brian turned in frustration to face the audience. "RING!"

Now he was frozen, his back to the flip chart, unable to move. After a painful minute or two of excruciating silence, Brian said, "I give up!"

I looked at my watch and noted the total elapsed time—five minutes. "Thank you," I said, "Excellent job! You did precisely what I had hoped. Go ahead and take your seat; I will tell you more about all this later."

"May I have another volunteer?" Now the audience froze. After a rather grim silence, a woman named Jean stood up resolutely. "Great!" I said, and I gave her instructions to leave the room as Brian had done earlier.

This time the group decided that our volunteer's task would be to walk up to the table near the lectern and pour a glass of water from a pitcher sitting on the water service tray. When Jean returned, I explained to her, "As with the last volunteer, the group has determined a task for you to perform. However, this time I will ring the bell EVERY TIME you do something *right*."

Receiving the reassuring ringing of the bell with each move in the direction of the water, Jean strode confidently to the front of the room. When she veered left, the bell stopped. This effectively swung her back to the right direction. She spotted the pitcher and walked up to it. Continuing to hear the bell's encouragement, she lifted the pitcher and poured a glass of water. When everyone in the room roared their approval (and disbelief), Jean turned to receive the applause. She went on to drink the water, which gave everyone a good chuckle.

"Door to pour—fifty-eight seconds!" I announced, glancing at my watch. Some audience members insisted there had to have been some kind of setup. With that, Jean poured a second and a third, handing one to Brian and one to me. We three raised our glasses to each other and to the audience in celebration.

Over the years, this demonstration predictably produces similar results. As the first person receives negative reinforcement from the bell, creativity and responsiveness go down—suppressed with a force proportionate to the number of times the bell rings. At the moment he gave up, Brian looked incompetent, totally stuck, and unable to respond.

On the other hand, when our second volunteer receives positive reinforcement from the bell, confidence, creativity, and success increase. Jean looked brilliant, confident, capable, and creative.

In truth, both people are capable. Both Brian and Jean—and you and I—were born into life as naturally brilliant learners with a wealth of creative reserves. What went wrong for Brian in my demonstration is exactly what goes wrong in many areas of our lives. The best way to get started on a goal when you clearly know that you are stuck is to first notice the oscillation. You cannot release if you are busily avoiding the fact that you are bouncing back and forth like crazy.

The chapters in Part 2 and Part 3 of this book will show you how to break out of oscillation, eliminate your stuck states, and switch on your Natural Brilliance. Before we get there, I invite you to understand your own stuck states clearly. Come to know the nature of your stuck states. Then get on the highroad to releasing your genius.

Diagnose Your Stuck State

Diagnosing your stuck state can help you release stress and notice more of what is going on in and around you. Notice how you keep your stuck state in place. Keep this self-survey and discovery interesting and fun. By diagnosing your stuck state, you dampen oscillation and prepare for responding in resourceful ways.

The questions below will help you gain insight into your present state. Go through them once lightly. Do not aim to be thorough here. This is not psychotherapy or analysis; this is an exploration of your current situation. Your objective will probably be to produce the results you want in life.

1) *What is the difference between your present state and your desired outcome? In what area of your life do you notice oscillation?* In the Natural Brilliance retreat we invite you to examine six areas of your life in which most people strive to achieve higher levels of fulfillment. These include:

- Work/Creating/Self-Expression
- Learning/Intellectual
- Physical Wellness
- Social/Interpersonal/Community
- Family/Personal
- Spiritual/Emotional

What recurrent pattern do you recognize in your behavior in one area of your life?

2) *What personal identity do you maintain in relationship to this issue? How do you view yourself, what do you affirm to yourself about this issue, and what do you believe to be true for you?*

For example, I used to have a dilemma with television. I viewed myself as a competent presenter in every other forum. "I don't feel comfortable in front of a camera. I have to play to a live audience because I take my cues from their responses. Give me a speaking opportunity, and I will be fine, lively, and animated. But, put me on TV, and I'm stilted and wooden." When you read Chapter 12 about the New Option Generator, you will learn how to change such a view.

3) *What is the predominant emotion?* Notice your feelings, your emotions in the stuck state. Feel the feelings you experience when you feel stuck. Label them.

4) *Using the information you have gathered from the first questions, what is your unresolvable paradox?* What opposing outcomes do you want at the same time? In my Toastmaster's example from Chapter 1, I wanted to develop my skills as a speaker, but I also wanted to avoid being at the lectern delivering my prepared speech. A way to phrase this is, "On the one hand I want X, but at the same time, on the other hand, I want Y."

This paradoxical problem is your stuck state. You can't stop and go at the same time.

5) *What are the benefits and detriments inside your paradox?* In Chapter 11, we will explore the Creative Problem-Solving process to gain insight into the nature of your stuck state. You will discover the benefits and detriments at each end of your current continuum of behavior. Without consciously realizing it, you have wanted to achieve the benefits at each end and avoid the detriments at each end, at the same time. It is the oscillation between these two simultaneously occurring, paradoxically opposed, unresolved states within you that defines your stuck state.

6) *What fears are associated with your stuck state?* Assuming that the truth about you is that you are infinitely resourceful, the fears are mythical, based on faulty conclusions that you failed earlier in life. Determine to confront your fears to get the breakthrough you need.

With Natural Brilliance you make the choice to no longer stop and go back when you face an emotional, intellectual, or physical stop sign. Your creative new choice can be to pause, gather new resources, and take action to achieve your goals.

Confront Your Stop Signs

Whatever you *now do successfully* in life is a model of successful learning. In the process of learning how to succeed, you naturally followed the steps of the Natural Brilliance model. At least one part of you was so focused on accomplishing the result that whatever happened was okay. If you failed to achieve a goal one day, you learned from it. The next day, a little smarter and more skilled, you took the next step. In this way you gained all you needed to ensure success.

Whatever you *seem unable to accomplish* in life is a model of a stuck state. Somewhere early in your life, as you attempted to use your natural learning capacities and accomplish your desires, you got "whacked" by a failure. The problem was not so much that you failed; the problem was the intensity of the whack. The whack was a sudden adverse stimulus or flood of negative feelings and thoughts. That whack planted a giant red octagonal stop sign in your path of learning. From then on, the stop sign operated emotionally, physically, or intellectually with the same ferocity as the original whack. Years later when you got the opportunity to do something in this area of your life, part of you wanted to proceed; part of you wanted to stop and pull back. You began to oscillate, which produced a stuck state—the inability to accomplish what you desired.

Do you recognize the scenario that causes the stuck state? Let us take the example of relationships. A boy wants to be friends with a girl at school. She gives him a powerful punch in the body-mind by saying, "Oooh, get away from me, you ugly creep!" Or a family member says, "You are so shy, I wonder how you will ever get to know anyone." In goes a stop sign. Many years later, the situation has changed, but the stop sign still looms over his emotional landscape. The boy, now a young man, wants to date but agonizes about asking women to go out with him.

We erect stop signs unconsciously as a neurological matter of survival to keep us from repeating dangerous actions. Even though survival is no longer at stake, the stop sign continues to function as if it were. Rather than helping us, the stop sign prevents us from living fully. The good news is, with Natural Brilliance, you can pull stop signs down when you want to learn and grow.

Balance with Your Counterbalance

Consider that almost everything about you operates with opposing forces. The construction of your musculature, nervous system, and personality all use opposing forces in a push-and-pull design. An elevator can serve as an analogy. Most elevators are built with a counterbalance, which moves opposite to the elevator. When the car goes up, the counterweight moves down—creating a two-phase, or *biphasic,* basis of operation. The biphasic design works to your benefit, as long as you use it properly.

A counterbalance ensures flexibility, allowing an elevator to stop at any position. You can think of a stuck state as the elevator car frozen between floors, the result of two equal forces, directly opposing each other. Stuck states in people result from the wrong use of our biphasic design. One force pulls, and the other responds with equal and opposite force, locking the body-mind into an internal tug-of-war.

Normal operation of our musculature involves extensor and flexor muscles used in controlled opposition. Our biphasic design allows us to move forward and back and stop anywhere in between. Similarly, our nervous system uses counterbalanced sympathetic and parasympathetic systems. The biphasic design gives us flexibility to experience emotions from love to fear and everything in between.

The human personality also has biphasic construction. For example, are you shy or bold? The answer is yes to both. It depends on the situation. You create a stuck state when you act overly shy or overly bold and remain that way. Choosing to live permanently at either end of a continuum can get us into trouble, because our survival depends on our ability to act and react flexibly across the entire range of behavioral and emotional options. Problems such as mental illness and physical disease occur when the personality, nervous system, or physical body gets locked into one way of living.

When we find a comfort zone, it makes sense that we would want to stop. But, life forces us to continue learning, growing, and changing with the accelerating changes in the world around us. We need to move ahead, and when part of us wants to stop, the resulting stuck state stops the learning process and the great rewards that life can offer.

You can change in all areas of your life where strong emotional, physical, or intellectual, stuck states have constricted or shut off learning. Pull down your stop signs with the steps of Natural Brilliance. You will eliminate stuck states because you instantly increase your options and make new, successful behaviors possible.

Notice Stuck States When They Happen

Over the next few days, watch people approach their stop signs. Observe everyone around you. Listen to what people say and watch the oscillation in their bodies. Notice their eyes when they hit a stop sign. You will see a characteristic double blink. With a blink, one picture flashes of what they want. They blink again, and the next picture flashes of their dysfunctional belief, what they do not want.

In hypnotic trance, the effects of oscillation become quite visible. When I was nineteen, I clearly saw oscillation between the states of *want* and *have*. I was fortunate to study hypnosis with Zula Bowers, a stage-hypnotist-turned-therapist. One day a church youth group called to request a demonstration of hypnosis. Zula taught me entertaining stage tricks I became eager to try.

"Once you have a subject in trance," she said, "suggest that he or she cannot do some simple act. For example, say to him he can't tell you his name, or suggest that his shoe is glued to the floor and he can't move it."

She leaned forward and explained with great emphasis, "Say the words, 'No matter how hard you try, you *cannot. Try,* you *cannot. Try!*' I guarantee, Paul, it will work." She was absolutely right. Once the inner mind of the subject had accepted the suggestion that he could not do something, no matter how hard he tried, he could not.

If you relate this to the biphasic construction of our physiology, one set of muscles is pushing with equal force as the opposing muscles are pulling. The result is a stuck state.

During my stage performance, I was awestruck as a six-foot man stood before me, with his foot "glued" to the floor, unable to tell me his name. Every part of him strained to perform the tasks that I had suggested and that he had accepted he could not do. The crowd was in hysterics. I was thinking to myself, "Whoa! We stop ourselves every single day. We are taking perfectly reasonable capacities and throwing them away because we honestly believe we *cannot.*"

The phrase *I can't* is the most powerful force of negation in the human psyche. Test its effect for yourself. In all those areas of your life where you feel stuck, can you also hear a recording that you have played over and over again to yourself and those around you? "No matter how hard I *try,* I *just can't* seem to..."

From the moment I saw that hypnotic subject struggle against himself on stage, I have devoted my professional life to freeing people from their self-imposed stuck states. My professional mission centers on creating learning opportunities for people to discover their vast resourcefulness. Then, I assist in their applying those resources to producing desired results in their lives. Natural Brilliance is the best way to quickly gain such benefits.

In your moments of trance, you may have experienced strong emotional learning in which you accepted a life sentence of negation. In those situations, you planted stop signs that have never come out. Discover how to pull out the stop signs and get back on the path to realizing your innate genius. The phrase *I can* will replace negation and point the way to new levels of achievement.

Learn from Others Getting Stuck

When I was in Portland, a PhotoReading instructor introduced me to a friend at the Beaverton Optometric Clinic, Dr. Roger Tabb. He is an optometrist specializing in Sensory Perceptual Training.

He took me through several experiences at the stations he had set up to help people overcome neurosensory stuck states. One station consisted of a trampoline. On the wall in front of me was a piece of paper with the words *THE BOY WENT HOME* written on it. Just below the sentence was the letter *X*.

In this exercise I was to bounce on the trampoline. Every time I got to the bottom of the bounce, I was to perform a task of calling out letters in a unique sequence.

After watching me botch the task three times, Dr. Tabb said, "I can tell exactly two bounces before you are going to make a mistake. You always bounce back on the trampoline about nine inches. At that moment, you break your concentration on the task to either review what you just did or to predict what's coming." I thought it amazing that my body communicated nonverbally to Dr. Tabb. He could see that my attempt to do the task properly actually prevented me from performing it.

Procrastination in the sales profession is another good example of oscillation that leads to stuck states. The salesperson wants to make the sale but does not want to be rejected. Rejection of himself or his product can throw him into an oscillation of "I can do this, but my product is no good" or "My product is good, but I can't do this. I'm no good at selling."

Procrastination, putting off calling customers, is a solution. Like many of our paradoxical solutions to oscillation, procrastination is a solution that sometimes makes things worse. Every time we procrastinate, we oscillate. We may want to achieve a goal, but we also want to avoid the pain of doing what it takes to achieve it. The more we avoid doing what it takes, the deeper we mire in our problem state.

In college I knew a student who had not graduated in the seven years she had attended classes. Sheila would only register for classes she was interested in. After a quarter or two, the counselor would urge her to take core courses, such as chemistry and math. Unfortunately, when she got a difficult assignment, she would put off doing it until it was too late. Invariably she ended up dropping out of all the classes she hated in a particular major, until she could no longer receive enough credits to complete that major.

In those seven years, Sheila had had at least that many declared or undeclared majors. Her strategy for going to college was antithetical to her graduating.

In another case, I met a young man who had never grown up. Being immature and letting his parents support him, Andrew never had to face the really tough issues of life. Consequently, he never committed himself to a course of action that produced anything more than a temporary high from his emotional dilemma.

When his father objected enough, Andrew would launch out on his own for a few months until he had failed at work and lost his job and, eventually, his apartment. Then he would go back home again, where he would spasmodically continue making weak commitments to live a self-sufficient life.

What could possibly break the cycles of failure plaguing Andrew, Sheila, and the sales procrastinators I described? Believe me, if you offered to help, you only increase their oscillation. The change must come from within, step-by-step, learning to take an easier path to success. The Steps of Natural Brilliance engender internal change, without pressure, while minimizing oscillation and increasing solutions. All the changes occur as a result of experiencing life fully.

Recognize Benefits and Dangers at Your Stop Sign

As we human beings naturally erect and preserve stop signs, we need to ask ourselves what the adaptive value is of each stop sign we encounter. What is the value of stopping when we want to progress?

Certainly, as children, we must learn from our mistakes. If a child steps into the street without looking, as I did, he is lucky to have someone stop his dangerous behavior fast. The problem is, when our stop sign is an emotional, psychological, neurophysiological, or intellectual wound, we stop learning effectively. Almost every adult I ever met has some early emotional wounding as a learner.

In one PhotoReading course a woman named Lisa was irate at me for her inability to get anything out of the course. Nothing she did seemed to be working. By the last session, she was in a rage. As the course opened that morning, she attacked me, the course, and Learning Strategies Corporation. Suddenly I could see her oscillation. There she was trying to learn something and unable to achieve the goal she wanted. Spotting this, I used my intuition to pull out the stop sign.

"You know what this reminds me of," I said, catching her off guard. "I remember a woman in my class one time who had a similar amount of anger when trying to learn PhotoReading. It turned out that in first grade her teacher had ridiculed her in front of the entire class because she made a mistake while reading out loud."

"Oh, my God," she said, as the furrow of anger in her brow widened to a look of stunned surprise. "That is exactly what happened to me in second grade." With her eyes unfocused, as if in a trance, she relived the moment when the stop sign was installed. "My second grade teacher stood in the front of the class and said to everyone, 'Lisa is never going to amount to anything in life because SHE CAN'T READ!'"

Everything Lisa had tried to do to improve her reading only reinforced the message she accepted at that moment in second grade. Whenever she could not do something in PhotoReading class, she faced her second grade teacher shrieking, "Lisa is never going to amount to anything!" Inside, Lisa was not the mature woman she appeared to be; she was the utterly helpless wounded second grader in a grownup's body.

Once Lisa connected her experience with my story, she broke the curse. She stopped her painful oscillation. Her Natural Brilliance restored, her genius went online. By the end of the final session of PhotoReading, Lisa was bubbling about going for her Master's Degree and looking forward to using PhotoReading to blast through the reading. "I know I can read fast!" she said proudly.

Dr. Buckminster Fuller wrote, in the introduction to a book about Maria Montessori's work, a powerful explanation of what challenges learning:

> All children are born geniuses. 9999 out of every 10,000 are
> swiftly, inadvertently, degeniused by grown-ups. This happens

because human beings are born naked, helpless, and—though superbly equipped cerebrally—utterly lacking in experience, therefore utterly ignorant. Their delicate sensing equipment is, as yet, untried. Born with built-in hunger, thirst, curiosity, the procreative urge, they can only learn what humanity has learned by trial and error—by billions upon billions of errors. Yet humanity is also endowed with self-deceiving pride. All those witnessing the errors of others proclaim that they (the witnesses) could have prevented those errors had they only been consulted. "People should not make mistakes," they mistakenly say. Motivated entirely by love, but also by fear for the futures of the children they love, parents, in their ignorance, act as though they know all the answers and curtail the spontaneous exploratory acts of their children, lest the children make "mistakes." But genius does its own thinking; it has confidence in its own exploratory findings, in its own intuitions, in the knowledge gained from its own mistakes. Nature has her own gestation rates for evolutionary development. The actions of parents represent the checks and balances of nature's gestation control. Humanity can evolve healthily only at a given rate.

Our culture has become obsessed with an educational system that wounds many types of learners. Perhaps those who mislabel students ought themselves to be called "teaching disabled."

Behold Opportunities beyond Your Stop Sign

Dr. Fuller personally told me one of his powerful life stories. Although he had achieved a high level of education, he had failed in business. As a father and husband, at 32, he realized he was never going to make it in life. He had bought society's negation of his genius and given up.

He walked to the bridge in town and stood on the railing ready to leap to his death. He then stopped and admitted to himself that he was a throwaway from society. As he knew himself to be completely worthless, he decided he would dedicate the rest of his life to an experiment.

His experiment, simply put, was "to find out just how much one little man could do for the planet." He was fifty years into his experiment when he told me of it.

He contributed numerous magnificent ideas and inventions. Perhaps he was best known to the public as the man who created the EPCOT Center geodesic dome at Disney World. A world-renowned architect, futurist, author, and inventor, he developed the field of geodesics. But, I know him for his natural brilliance.

"Bucky" Fuller showed me a key to finding Natural Brilliance. Believe in people's dreams and say, "*You CAN!*"

I know how swiftly and inadvertently we are degeniused in childhood by well-intentioned but misguided people influencing our lives. A symptom of how this affects us is clear: we have goals we are trying hard to achieve; yet, year after year, we continue to perpetuate stuck states.

In the last two decades I have come to know that it is as easy to learn effectively as it is to get stuck. Once you know how you accept and erect stop signs into your life, you will find it remarkably simple and more productive to create what you want in life.

The rest of this book is devoted to showing you how to let your Natural Brilliance shine to create what you want whenever and wherever you run into an oscillation or stuck state. In the four-step model called Natural Brilliance, you can acquire the methods for pulling out the stops and having "ALL SYSTEMS GO!" You can reclaim the truth about yourself as a learner. Life is for fun and learning. Natural Brilliance makes all learning fun and turns all fun into learning. Enjoy!

> **What stops most people in their tracks is a small mental packet of energy. It is called a thought. They think "I can't."**
>
> **Rex Steven Sikes**
> **Founder of IDEA Seminars**

> **Any strength in the wrong context can be a weakness.**

3

The Heart of Natural Brilliance

Enter Part 2 of this book with caution. You will learn the skills of Natural Brilliance in the next four chapters, and an even bigger opportunity awaits you as well. Thinking of Natural Brilliance as practicing four steps is like trying to drink from a dripping faucet when a waterfall is cascading in front of you. You can gain immediate benefits with this model if you approach it as more than a set of techniques for self-development. Recognize the inherent power of mind harnessed by the Natural Brilliance model, and you will do much more than overcome stuck states or gain access to the capacities for genius you now possess. You can cross the threshold to manifest your highest good in life. In the remaining chapters of Part 2, we will explore each step in depth to ensure you have the skills to apply them successfully.

The Natural Brilliance model is founded on five principles that match the world's most powerful and effective human development approaches. It effectively resolves paradoxical problems, guiding relaxed, incremental changes to increase your options. It is a model for "being to do," thus breaking the "do-to-be" compulsion of our culture. Natural Brilliance maintains a powerful outcome orientation, keeping your full resources engaged in the most efficient ways for achieving your goals. Finally, it takes a generative approach to human development and change. Here are the Natural Brilliance principles:

Principle 1: Tolerate ambiguity to realize your full potential.
Principle 2: Make small adjustments slowly to accomplish your goal.
Principle 3: Achieve a state of being by *being*, not *doing*.
Principle 4: Maintain an outcome orientation and increase choices.
Principle 5: Change in generative ways for the best results.

Principle 1:
Tolerate Ambiguity to Realize Your Full Potential

If I ask "Are you strong-willed or easygoing," what would you say? You would probably answer "Yes" because, although I phrased the question as an alternative, in truth, you have the choice of acting out both extremes and anything between. As a capable, mature human being, you know that circumstances will influence how you act. Although you may have a preference, in reality, you can act strong or easygoing as necessary.

On a continuum of behavioral options, strong-willed forms one endpoint and easygoing forms its opposite. Many people learn to live within certain parameters on any one continuum of options. For example, if you are too strong-willed, you may act overly assertive or obstinate, either forcing people or refusing to compromise. Similarly, if you are too easygoing, people could use you as a doormat or take advantage of you. You have consciously and unconsciously defined a range you can comfortably live within.

Many people were on hand to guide your defining your range of choices. Those in authority told you, "This way to behave is proper; that is not." They put a stop sign in front of you whenever you behaved inappropriately. Once you had established your "safety zone," seldom if ever did you venture beyond the endpoints of that continuum. The comfort zone between the stop signs became the unconscious limit of choices you consciously even considered exercising.

In effect, you may still be forcing all other choices of behaving to stand outside the stop signs, including your disenfranchised creative self. The natural learning behaviors you used to explore your world in childhood may still be relegated to a place out of view to those around you and often even to yourself.

With Natural Brilliance you can rediscover you are not one way or the other. The secret to joyous learning is to recognize a wide range of choices emotionally, physically, and intellectually. Thinking about them is not enough to retrain our nervous systems. You need to exercise choices you may have held at bay for decades.

In Chapter 12, Natural Brilliance steps are sequenced into a change process called the *New Option Generator*. Using it, you can locate the stop signs unconsciously installed in your life and pop them out. To eliminate oscillation, you can vaporize the endpoints on the continuum between behavioral opposites. You can begin integrating your options for responding on the entire spectrum of choices. All the choices you could not have considered before suddenly become fully available to you. With the New Option Generator you can reclaim your creative potential.

Principle 2:
Make Small Adjustments Slowly to Accomplish Your Goal

Everything about learning to fly is unusual. Flying is a perfect laboratory to study people trying to cope with an unstable environment.

One exercise in pilot's training requires a special visor-like contraption worn as a hood to prevent seeing outside the cockpit of the airplane. The hood only allows a view of the front instrument panel. The objective of the exercise is to train people to fly only by the information from your instruments, not by other information their sensory systems might erroneously interpret.

During the exercise, the flight instructor has student pilots change heading and altitude and make many other minor adjustments. The typical response is to overcontrol the plane. If a slight adjustment in heading of five degrees is required, the tension in the student's body and the lack of sensitivity to the controls will cause the student to over-correct by two or three times what is necessary. Overcontrolling an airplane throws it into an oscillation, which tends to worsen the situation by swinging it past the desired goal.

The experienced pilot makes small, incremental adjustments with relaxed patience. There is a sense of confidence about the flight—there will be enough time. Relax. Everything is going to be fine.

The harder you try to get unstuck, the more difficult your task. Paradoxically, trying harder tends to make the stuck state much worse.

Take the example of a relationship problem. Trying hard to convince people not be angry tends to make them angrier. In other words, when you push harder to handle one side of a problem, you end up increasing the swing that keeps you oscillating. The more you oscillate, the farther you move from a solution.

When an airplane is nose-diving toward the ground, most student pilots try to pull out. Their panic only puts the airplane into a spin—a much more perilous situation. Paradoxically, to pull the airplane out, the pilot has first to push gently into the dive. Then air flows over the wings properly to create lift under the wing so that the plane can resume flying. Then the pilot can slowly pull back to take the plane out of the dive.

Pulling out of a nose dive successfully offers a hint on how to handle almost any other situation where oscillation occurs. Make small adjustments is part of the solution. Three additional principles follow.

Principle 3:
Achieve a State of Being by *Being* Not *Doing*

If I asked you "What do you want to achieve," what would you say? The goal you stated would be a desired result you want to create for yourself or your family.

If I kept asking the question, you would begin to identify the goals that exist behind your most obvious goal. What do you suppose you would find out after several minutes of my asking "If you accomplished *that goal*, what even *more important* goal would you then want to achieve?" That question elicits a chain of outcomes as you continue to search for additional answers. At the end of your chain of outcomes waits your *real* goal, the end goal, not goals that are means to the end. Natural Brilliance has a way of gently coaxing your core goal into consciousness.

For example, in PhotoReading, we ask participants to tell us what they want to achieve during the course. One person in each course invariably says, "I want to master the techniques of PhotoReading." I then ask this person to participate in a demonstration of eliciting a chain of outcomes. The demonstration involves my asking, after each goal statement, "If you accomplished *that goal*, what even *more important* goal would you then want to achieve?" The chain of outcomes I elicited during one demonstration went as follows:

First Goal: Master the techniques of PhotoReading
- Be able to converse with people at work with a level of expertise on various important topics
- Get promoted and earn more money
- Provide for the well-being and happiness of my family
- See my children grow up into happy, healthy, capable adults
- Experience the fullness of my own potential

Core goal: Total "beingness," a feeling of total peace

In this example, as with all the examples of this exercise, the bottom line is a *core state* of being.

All of the goals in the chain of goals are really means to the desired result. Often, people accomplish a goal yet feel unfulfilled. Of course. They were really trying to get another goal. Here is the interesting dilemma: Goals are things that you *do*, whereas the real result is a state of *being*. The *doing* is a means to an end.

The problem most people face is that they are unaware of the goal behind their goals. As a result they get fixated on *doing* to be and never get to where they want to *be*. Many people imagine that if only they could succeed at completing their outcome chain, they would then gain access to the state they desire. Unfortunately, few people ever complete their outcome chain. Those who do accomplish several of their goals in their chain of outcomes soon discover the emptiness of *doing* to *be*.

Once guided through a process of examining their inner motivations, people recognize that the goal behind their goals is the achievement of a core state—an experience of full aliveness. They express it as "beingness," "completeness," or "okay-ness."

It seems we have a cultural imperative that to experience a better state of being, you must earn it by doing things better. The result of that imperative is oscillation, a stuck state that many people compulsively try to resolve unsuccessfully. They have a struggle because the only way to fully *be* is to experience yourself as a human *being*, not as a "human doing."

Connirae Andreas, in her book *Core Transformations,* suggests that we reverse the outcome chain to enhance the way we do everything in life. Start with the state of being, then you will be much more capable and efficient at all the actions you choose to do in life.

Her process brilliantly breaks through the oscillation from "do" to "be." Think back to the example chain of outcomes from PhotoReading, and it will make sense. In truth, course participants will be capable of achieving their goals in the chain if they approach their goals with a sense of "total 'beingness,' a feeling of peace."

Breaking the "do-to-be" paradox is an integral part of the Natural Brilliance model. I will show you how to approach Step 3, Respond, from a powerful state of being. The decisiveness and commitment of such a state focuses your personal power for effective action and success.

Principle 4:
Maintain an Outcome Orientation and Increase Choices

Another key principle of the Natural Brilliance model is that you can facilitate your learning by concentrating not on problems but on outcomes. This keeps the mind, the most perfect goal-seeking device, oriented on achieving what you want rather than creating what you do not want.

Dwelling on our problems is like trying to drive forward in a car looking only in the rearview mirror. We tend to think of the limitations that the problems create. It is easy to notice blocks, lack of resources, mistakes, and blame. Consequently, we will most likely generate bad feelings and rack ourselves with either guilt about the past or anxiety about the future.

In general, focusing on problems is a sure way to continue the oscillation of your stuck state. On the other hand, focusing on outcomes gets you to imagine possibilities. By keeping your gaze high while driving, you can respond to more of the passing vistas. From the perspective of the long view, reviewing and exploring the past helps generate curiosity and learning, giving you clues to success.

An outcome orientation increases the number of paths you can take. The Natural Brilliance model uses an outcome orientation in the steps of Noticing, Responding, and Witnessing to ensure each step you take leads to higher learning.

Principle 5
Change in Generative Ways for the Best Results

The Natural Brilliance model is a generative model for learning and human development. It does more than fix the existing problem; it fixes the way you created the problem in the first place. If you sat on a tack, you would not run to a doctor for morphine to mask the pain. That is remedial change which seeks to remedy the immediate symptoms of the problem. Remedial change is the opposite of generative change. Many therapeutic models try to find remedies for problems.

Generative change means that the process of changing a problem generates its own learning for future situations. The generative way to remove pain if you sit on a tack is to pull the tack out.

Remedial change tends to put energy into increasing oscillation. Natural Brilliance minimizes oscillation and strengthens the learner with each cycle of the process.

When I consult with businesses, my job is to train my clients in how I do what I do, effectively replacing myself and working myself out of a job. I teach generative change. Natural Brilliance, as a model of generative change, encourages you to seek the most elegant and efficient ways to become stronger each day. Whenever you face a problem situation with Natural Brilliance, you increase your problem-solving skills.

Take a Brilliant Approach to Life and Enjoy the Benefits

In the next five chapters you will learn the steps of the Natural Brilliance model, taking the knowledge and skills into your process of growth and development. Engaging in this learning model, you will enjoy benefits right away. You will find that Natural Brilliance:

- Naturally minimizes the oscillation of your current stuck states.
- Allows for incremental shifts towards specific outcomes.
- Focuses on you as a competent, capable learner.
- Allows you to witness your unfolding genius.
- Increases awareness of personal strengths.
- Eliminates guilt for failing to accomplish a goal.
- Eliminates performance anxiety as you learn.

In Chapter 1, you gained an overview of the Natural Brilliance model and the techniques you can use to achieve immediate results. Chapter 2 explained stop signs, oscillations, and stuck states. It invited you to explore where you wanted to break through and gain access to your genius potential. Chapter 3 has described the five principles of Natural Brilliance so you can confidently use the model to accomplish your goals.

Now that the overview is complete, you can guide your conscious and nonconscious mind through the process to reclaim your Natural Brilliance. Ready! Set! Pull out those stop signs and let's Go!

4

Release

Think of how your day would go if you took a balanced and relaxed approach to the events you encountered. When you relax, you expand your sensory awareness to process useful information. Relaxation increases the sensitivity of your physical receptors and enhances your fine motor control, allowing you to move effectively and efficiently. When you are relaxed, you can also enter expanded brain states and gain access to the resources of your nonconscious mind to increase learning and choices. Perhaps most important of all, approaching your day in a relaxed way permits emotional and cognitive flexibility essential to thriving in our chaotic modern times. Step 1, Release, gives you the balanced and relaxed state you need for success.

Your best performance begins with the release of conflicting thoughts, emotions, or behaviors. Eliminating unnecessary oscillation and focusing your body-mind results in releasing stress and tension. Unless they are acutely stressed, most clients I work with do not recognize how tension controls their bodies and limits their thinking process. In this chapter we will find hidden physical and mental tension and develop skills to release.

Discover Tension

The opposite of release is tension. If you watch a large cat prowling its natural habitat, you see the difference. The cat's gaze diverges, and its pupils dilate to absorb information from all around. Then, when something catches its attention, instantaneously its pupils constrict, its eyes focus, and its body goes on alert.

The same is true for you. When the systems of your body and mind tense, they undergo a natural physiological and psychological effect. Your sensory systems tend to narrow. Your hearing, feeling, and thinking focus. Limited input from your senses allows you to concentrate on one thing at a time. Because your emotional and cognitive choices are also limited, you stay on target, free from distracting or conflicting thoughts.

Unfortunately, in the Information Age, such responses to tension work against us. We are required to solve problems and make decisions continually; to make effective decisions, we need to take in information freely. If we worry about problems and decisions, our problem-solving and decision-making abilities constrict.

Another negative by-product of a lot of tension is its effects on physical performance. Tension in muscles forces us to use large muscle groups, which work harder without coordinated use of fine motor skills. Large muscle actions cause us to over-compensate and over-control. Performance goes down.

A classic example of this performance barrier shows up with people who are trying to perform at entry-level standards for jobs; such as stenography, zip code sorting, and typing. Students for these jobs can consciously learn all the skills they need to perform the tasks. However, to pass a test, they have to release to get incoming information. Their bodies must respond faster than their conscious mind can think, so the students have to let go of conscious awareness to move at rates only the inner mind can produce.

Unfortunately, when the time comes for proficiency testing, many students tense and try too hard. They fail to perform as well as they have learned, let alone fast enough to pass the test.

Take a moment to feel in your own body how tension creates problems:

Gently tense your calves, thighs, stomach, back, shoulders, and face. Take a breath and hold it for a moment. How do you feel? How long do you think you can last like this?

Now release the breath and all the tension. Notice what happens in your body, your breath, your mind. The natural response to tension is release. What do you do when you come home after a hard day? If you have a free moment, you probably take a deep breath and exhale with a sigh as you sit down. As you do, you spontaneously release your shoulders, stomach, and back. What do you experience after release?

At the end of your day, when you first lie down and put your head on the pillow, don't you feel wonderful? Permission to release comes when you say to yourself "I have nothing to do but rest." The body restores and revitalizes all the systems of the body and mind, replenishing depleted reserves.

I do not want to mislead you. The means to increased human performance is not to relax totally. Too little tension leads to inertia and boredom. Studies for decades have shown that our systems need some tension for optimum performance.

Researcher and author Mihalyi Csikzentmihalyi refers to a "delicate zone between boredom and anxiety" as the "flow state." Herbert Benson, Harvard medical doctor and researcher, has demonstrated that breaking the "anxiety cycle" can be accomplished by initiating the "Relaxation Response." PhotoReading uses the flow state for information processing with written materials. While PhotoReading, the whole mind switches on, bringing readers into an enhanced state and making remarkable capacities available to them. The goal of Release is to bring the body and mind into an ideal state for performing.

Release: From Tension to Relaxation

Many things cause us to tense and keep us from using our full range of resources. Any stimulus outside that we interpret as dangerous will set off an anxiety cycle. Oftentimes, a stimulus in our environment that reminds us of a negative past event automatically throws us into a defensive response.

Sometimes we tense at television and other media bombarding our senses. We can become habituated to living in a state of tension so that we hardly realize we are carrying tension in our low back or abdomen or across the back of our neck.

As many paths lead to tension, so many paths lead to relaxation. Numerous simple techniques can help us achieve instant relaxation.

Once I spoke about instant relaxation techniques at the noon meeting of a local Rotary Club. After demonstrating a ninety-second technique on six volunteers, I opened the floor for discussion. One of the volunteers interjected, "Before you get into this discussion, I want to share something."

The man pulled two pink pieces of paper out of his tweed blazer pocket and continued. "These are two prescriptions for tranquilizers. I received them from my doctor today. I just realized I don't need them because, in that ninety seconds, I became more relaxed than I had been for the last six months. I wanted to let you know."

Deep physical and mental relaxation is no miracle. It is always one thought away from your present state. You will learn to produce an optimum state of relaxation very quickly by following the instructions of this chapter.

In his book *Autogenic Training*, Kai Kermani outlines numerous techniques for getting into the ideal state of relaxation. His approaches center around several simple principles:

- Work with your thoughts. Calm thoughts lead to a calm mind and body.
- Deal with emotions. Emotions are thought-energy in motion in your physical body. Learn to let emotions as they wash over you give way to calmness.
- Change your physiology. Physiology leads your emotional state and creates the platform for mental and emotional relaxation.
- Exercise your major muscle groups. In addition to releasing pent-up tension, exercise causes the brain to release neurochemicals that are mood altering in positive ways.

Develop Skills

If you study relaxation techniques, you will notice a pattern emerging. It does not matter if you are emotionally tense, mentally wired, or physically stressed; the rule is the same: Physiology First.

When you change your physiology, you change everything. As you learned earlier in this chapter, when you take a deep breath and soften your shoulders and posture, you initiate relaxation. Relaxation is where you start any technique of Release.

Let me give you an illustration. If someone held my nose and mouth so that I could not breathe, after a minute or two my body would begin to tense up and struggle to get oxygen. If I were still conscious after three minutes, I would be frantically flailing my arms and body in an attempt to get free.

Breath invisibly links body and brain. When you change your breathing, you change your mental and physical states. Try it:

Take a deep breath and let it go. Now relax so that you inhale and exhale evenly. Breathe a complete cycle without any pauses between the inhale and exhale. Imagine breathing a circle in which one breath flows evenly into the next without jerk or pause. Take thirty seconds to close your eyes and continue to breathe in that way; notice the effect circular breathing has on your body and mind.

You probably recognized that when you relaxed your breathing, you simultaneously and spontaneously relaxed your body and mind. When you relaxed the link between the two, body and mind follow suit. The corresponding changes in your body and mind also change your emotions.

Choose Excellence

If you want to change a stuck state, first change your physiology. Release, and everything positive will ripple out from this shift.

Here is a way to change state to get resources quickly:

Stand, slouch your shoulders forward, and lower your head. Stiffen your right knee and shift your weight to your right heel. Let your arms dangle. This is the physiology of depression. Make your breathing shallow. Now think a depressing thought, something such as a major mistake you experienced once a long time ago.

Now that you feel depressed, I will guide you to release in thirty seconds or less. Ready?

Take a deep breath as you straighten your spine, raise your head, and straighten your shoulders. Exhale as you center your weight over both feet, shoulder-width apart. Move one foot slightly ahead of the other, and tilt your weight to the balls of your feet. Breathe evenly with a full, deep abdominal and chest breath. This is the physiology of excellence. Now remember a major success.

How do you feel? Notice the differences between depressed and excellent? The physiology of excellence will successfully change your emotional state one hundred percent of the time, because physiology leads emotions. So, if you find yourself in the doldrums or in a stuck state, know that you can change within thirty seconds. Assume

the physiology of excellence. Simply standing up and breathing differently will make an instant difference in your mental attitude. Accessing a powerful physiology and positive mental image will make you resourceful.

Anchor the Relaxation Response

Each and every time you experience a state of true release, anchor it. Anchoring is the process of assigning a stimulus to a response. The concept of Conditioned Response training was first introduced by the Russian psychologist, Pavlov, in his famous experiments with dogs.

The anchor you set can be physical, auditory, visual, or any combination. For example, a physical anchor could be squeezing your right hand into a fist and releasing it. If you link this squeeze and release to a relaxing experience, then squeezing and releasing of your fist anytime in the future will spontaneously trigger a similar state of relaxation. The more often you repeat the anchor, the more powerful it becomes.

An auditory anchor could be internally stating a word or phrase, such as "excellent" or "calm and poised." A visual anchor could be seeing an internal image of a religious symbol or picturing yourself succeeding.

Anchoring is an effective and simple technique. Use it as you play with the following exercises.

Relax in Ninety Seconds

Remember the story I told earlier of my presentation to Rotarians? Well, here is how the demonstration goes. You can try it by yourself or with a friend.

> Sit in a chair with your feet flat on the floor and your hands separated, resting palms up and open on your thighs. Take a deep breath, and as you exhale, close your eyes and think of the word *Relax* repeating in a space behind your eyes. Think only of the word *Relax*. Within ninety seconds, you will be very relaxed.
>
> An additional step is to imagine that your dominant arm and hand are as loose and as limply relaxed as a silk cloth. Then reach over with your nondominant hand and pick up the wrist of your dominant arm about six inches and let it plop down

on your thigh. (This is a bit easier to do for someone else, but it does work when you do it on yourself.)

After relaxing just as long as you like, bring your awareness once again outward by mentally counting forward from *1* to *5*, then opening your eyes, taking a deep breath, and stretching your arms.

It really is as simple as that. Try it!

Relax Deeper

The main technique to achieve deep relaxation is called "progressive relaxation," which involves moving your awareness from muscle group to muscle group.

As you focus your attention on any one part of your body, imagine that those muscles are becoming loose and limply relaxed. By the time you have gone from head to toe or toe to head, you will be profoundly relaxed.

Experiment with this:

> Direct your attention to the big toe of your right foot. Become aware of it. Good. Become aware of the heel of your left foot. Now become aware of your right kneecap. Good. Can you become aware of your left elbow? Now, direct your attention to your nostrils. Become aware of the flow of your breath coming into your nostrils as you inhale and flowing out of your nostrils as you exhale.

You directed your attention from place to place on your body. By doing so, you shut out any irrelevant stimuli that might have caused your body and mind to be involved and tense. Sneaky, eh?

Now that you have the idea, let me give you a detailed script to follow. Feel free to make a recording of it in your own voice. Or, have someone read it to you. You may also choose to listen to a professionally produced relaxation session, such as my *Deep Relaxation* Paraliminal.

The following process of relaxation takes 10 to 15 minutes. If you glance over the text now, when you have time to play with the process, you may choose to go through it thoroughly. It is the process of relaxation we teach PhotoReading students to develop deeply attuned states of learning with one deep breath. Over the course of training the participants learn the pattern for releasing, which can be used any time.

> Take a deep breath...hold it for a moment...as you slowly
> exhale, close your eyes. Think of the number *3*, and mentally
> repeat the word *Relax*. Imagine a wave of relaxation flowing
> downward throughout your entire body, from the top of your
> head down to the soles of your feet.

A wave of relaxation can begin at the top of your head and
begin to flow slowly, downward, across the muscles of your scalp,
flowing down through the forehead, relaxing all the muscles
around the eyes, nostrils, cheeks...flowing across the muscles
of your mouth, chin, and jaw. Relaxing down through the
muscles of your face, this wave can flow down through your
throat and neck and out across your shoulders. Imagine this
wave of relaxation flowing over the tops of your shoulders, the
front and back of your shoulders, and down your sides. This
wave can flow down your arms relaxing your upper arms, lower
arms, hands, fingers, and fingertips.

Imagine this wave of relaxation flowing right out your
fingertips, carrying any tight, tense feelings out and away.
You may even notice a pleasant tingling or vibrating sensation
on the tips of your fingers, as all the muscles relax deeper.

This pleasant wave of relaxation flows from your shoulders
down through the muscles of your chest and upper back.
Imagine this wave spreading gently and evenly throughout the
muscles of your chest and back, relaxing your breathing and all
around your heart. Notice the even rhythm and beating of your
heart as you relax around your heart. If your mind wanders,
you can gently, ever so gently, bring it back to what you are
doing here. There is plenty of time later for other thoughts.
Right now you are deeply relaxing.

Relaxing the heart, the muscles of the chest, imagine this
wave flowing down through your abdomen and throughout
all the organs of your body. Imagine the wave flowing down
your back, down through the middle and lower back. Imagine

this wave flowing slowly downward into your pelvis and hips. Relax down through the muscles of your legs, allowing this wave to flow throughout your thighs, calves, all the way down through your legs, right down to your ankles and feet. Relax your heels and toes, the tops and bottoms of your feet. Imagine this wave of relaxation flowing right out the bottoms of your feet, carrying any tensions out, flowing away, melting away. You may notice the curious sensation on the bottoms of your feet, as waves of relaxation carry your body into the level of comfort that is right for you. You are in charge.

Anytime you desire to relax as deep or deeper than you are now, you may do so by thinking of your physical relaxation signal, the number *3* and the word *Relax*. You are in charge.

{Pause}

Take another deep breath... hold it a moment...slowly exhale, think of the number *2* and mentally repeat the word *Relax*. Let go of thoughts about the past or future, focus your awareness on this present moment in time, right here, right now.

Imagine with each exhale that you are letting go of any fears, worries, problems of any kind. Exhale and let them go.

{Pause for a breath}

With each inhale, imagine inhaling relaxation, tranquillity, and comfort into every part of you.

{Pause for a breath}

So that with each breath you breathe, you let go more and relax even deeper. Imagine your consciousness expanding into this present moment.

Whenever you desire to relax as deep or deeper than you are now, you may do so by thinking of the number *2* and mentally repeating the word *Relax*.

Outside sounds that are unimportant to you... can help you to relax even deeper.

{Pause}

Take another deep breath in… hold it for a moment…slowly exhale, mentally hear the sound of the number *1* and imagine looking at a beautiful plant or flower.

{Pause}

This is a signal indicating that you have focused your awareness within, to this accelerated learning state. Here you have access to expanded creativity and perceptual ability. You are in contact with the abundant resources of your inner mind.

If you would like, imagine yourself relaxing in a beautiful quiet scene, sitting or lying back in a peaceful scene, relaxing and enjoying this time of comfort.

{Pause}

This is the ideal time to give yourself the positive affirmations that help you achieve the learning you desire. Right now, as you enjoy this relaxed internal state, give yourself positive and constructive affirmative statements that help you develop the Natural Brilliance step of Release.

For example, say to yourself, "I can achieve what I sincerely set my mind on. I believe in myself and willingly accept my full potential as a learner."

At your own rate, imagine giving yourself praises—some positive phrases to help you achieve what you desire. Hear them in your own mind as if you were saying them to yourself in your own inner voice.

When you are ready, begin to bring yourself out to an outer, consciously aware state of mind.

Using a standard procedure, you will be bringing yourself to the outer conscious level of awareness by the counting forward from *1* to *5*.

With each number, imagine yourself returning to outer awareness, carrying with you the good feelings of relaxation and alertness that you have developed. And at the last number, you open your eyes feeling refreshed, relaxed and alert— feeling good.

Now, at a rate that is comfortable for you, bring yourself out by the standard procedure of counting forward from 1 to 5. Take all the time you desire to return now.

Summary

You probably realize that releasing is as easy to do as exhaling deeply. When you guide your body and mind properly, every part of you is capable of relaxing. Over the next few days take opportunities to pace your busy life with a few moments of relaxation. You will quickly train yourself to release spontaneously in any situation, because you know you can.

When you face stress-producing situations, the knowledge and skills you develop with Step 1, Release, will benefit you immediately. In addition, when dealing with things that used to put you into stuck states, relax yourself and become playful. By using the techniques of this chapter, you will develop essential skills naturally. Each day, consider using one or more of the suggested ideas listed below until you have experienced all of them. Put a check mark in the box to indicate your progress:

Action Checklist for Release

- ❑ Physiology First: Breathe in complete, even cycles for thirty seconds, and notice the effect on your body and mind.
- ❑ Excellence: Get into a balanced, powerful physiology of excellence, and bring a positive memory to mind.
- ❑ Relaxation Anchor: Experience the state of release, then anchor it physically, auditorially, and/or visually.
- ❑ Ninety-Second Relaxation: Sit comfortably, release a deep breath, and focus your mind on the word *Relax* repeating behind your eyes. Feel your arm relaxed like a silk cloth.
- ❑ Deep Relaxation: Follow the script for progressive relaxation from head to toe.

Refer to the *Appendix* for additional tips.

5

Notice

Noticing, Step 2 of Natural Brilliance, puts your sensory systems back online when they have been switched off due to tension and oscillation. When your senses turn on, a wealth of valuable information becomes available, giving you new options for success. The experience of bringing your senses back online can be startling, like stepping out of a dark tunnel with the whole world opening vividly before you.

Twenty hours into my training as a private pilot, my instructor asked me to fly to the neighboring Anoka County airport. For weeks I had been obsessed with making sure every detail was correct while I was flying. I would frequently scan my six instruments to confirm I was on course and at the right altitude. I would look left and right over the two wings to make sure I was flying straight. I would check the horizon with a mark on my windshield to make sure I was flying level.

"Straight and level, all instruments check," I would mentally repeat to myself. This scanning routine dominated my consciousness every time I took to the air. But on this particular day, something unusual took place that changed my experience of flying forever.

As we approached the airport, I suddenly realized that I could see everything around me. All traffic for 15 miles was visible to me. I knew the exact approach of my airplane in relationship to the configuration of the runways. I could check in with all six instruments at one glance. I did not have to look left and right. The wings were like extensions of my own shoulders, and I knew they were level by simply looking ahead at my destination.

"Wow!" I said to my instructor, seated to my right. "This is amazing!

It's as if I can see everything all at once."

Mr. Hlusak smiled back and said, "Congratulations, you have removed your flight blinders."

Removing flight blinders happens for all pilots at some point. The domination of the limited conscious processing of the analytical mind suddenly gives way, and the whole mind switches on to panoramic vista.

The goal of Notice is to switch on the panoramic vista in your world. Let's get those flight blinders off.

Step Out of Your Tunnel

Whenever we are trying too hard to live life perfectly, we switch off the vast resources of the whole mind. As a result we live our lives with tunnel vision. We habituate ourselves to viewing the world through tunnel vision until we no longer realize how limited our perceptions are.

My brother Lee got glasses when he was eight years old. Neither he nor my parents knew how desperately nearsighted he was. The experience of stepping into the world with clear long vision amazed him.

As he describes it, "I had never known that grass is made up of individual blades. I thought it was one big green undifferentiated blob. Same with trees. I did not realize they had individual leaves until that day I stepped out of the optician's office."

When our sensory systems are diminished or down, we do not realize that the world around us carries information we need. Tunnel vision can be our obstacle to development; we do not know the effect of wearing blinders until they finally come off.

Notice More to Survive and Thrive

After draining stress out of our systems with Step 1, Release, we restore a natural sensitivity to our sensory systems. This makes the remarkable faculties of the brain fully available and permits us to make necessary discriminations to achieve our goals.

Step 2, Notice, is absolutely critical to our success in the world—literally, to our survival—and also to our ability to thrive in the modern age. Look at various cultures in the world that had to survive in harsh environments, and you shall see an interesting pattern: survival equals the ability to make wise decisions based on sensory distinctions.

Perhaps you have heard about the Eskimo people's ability to distinguish different types of snow. You and I might know seven or eight types, whereas the Inuit, as they prefer to be called, make over fifty distinctions. It is logical that if your life depended on discriminating one snow condition from another, you would certainly do so carefully. Imagine driving across country and not being able to tell one road sign from another. Dangerous proposition, no?

If you study the Nordic people, you will find a similar pattern of sensory awareness. They had a fairly small working vocabulary for everything concerning inland existence. When it came to words describing coastal regions—coves, rocks, waves, and other water conditions—they used dramatically more terms. Nordic people made remarkably fine discriminations regarding water, upon which they depended, and their success grew from these discriminations.

Now turn to you and me. We live in the Information Age in modern society. We must extract meaning from data and the world around us to make decisions for effective action. When we drive cars, information comes at us quickly. Lawyers, computer scientists, medical doctors, and other professionals need to process enormous amounts of information to keep up in their fields. What are the sensory distinctions we should be making to survive and thrive? How can we notice what we should be paying attention to in order to live our lives fully today?

Take the First Step toward Balance

By sharpening your awareness of the world around you and your own sensations in response, you will get rid of disorientation and find balance. I mentioned in Chapter 1 that the step of Notice creates an "outside of yourself" awareness. I used the analogy of hopping off the teeter-totter instead of trying to balance by running on the top of it from one end to the other. Achieving a perspective outside the oscillating system helps you to dampen the wild swings and bring the teeter-totter into balance.

Flight navigation is based on the same principle of balance. Even if you know where you started and where you are headed, you do not know where you are on the connecting path until you establish a third reference point. Knowing where you are with respect to a third point lets you plot an intersecting line, which gives you your position between where you are and where you are going.

Orienting requires triangulation. Balance requires it. Noticing creates it. To diminish either/or, this-not-that type of thinking that creates oscillation, get perspective. When you have another point of view away from the teeter-totter, you can discover what you have been doing and what other choices might get you where you want to go. Noticing allows you to get rid of the negative effects of disorientation to achieve the balanced sensation of knowing what to do next.

Increase Your Sensory Acuity

You perceive inside and all around you with your five physical senses. You use the visual and auditory senses, the sense of touch to perceive energy and motion, plus the senses of smell and taste. The way to enhance your sensory acuity is to increase your ability to notice changes in your environment. Your brain registers change, even minutely subtle changes in your environment. As you actively notice what your brain perceives, you will increase your sensory acuity.

Right now, while you are reading these words, notice what you feel on the back of your thighs. What is the temperature of your scalp? What is happening to the index finger of your right hand? What sounds do you hear that you have not been noticing until now?

You actively directed your attention to your various sensory systems. Perhaps you perceived a number of completely trivial bits of information. That's great. See how easy it is to notice what you have not been noticing up until now.

For every external sensory system, we have a corresponding internal representation. These representations are the operating system, or language, of the brain. We can enhance our internal sensory awareness as we can our external senses. Our ability to process information, make effective decisions, and, ultimately, succeed in society also depends on making internal sensory distinctions. The rest of this chapter helps you develop your external and internal sensory acuity.

Enhance Your Visual Sense

Imagine a visual input channel that can route information directly into your inner mind. Once there, your mind can sort through the data and deliver answers to you consciously whenever you want or need them. Would that be great? Well, guess what? You were born with the equipment to do just that.

The PhotoReading whole mind system is built on the idea that you have a nonconscious mind and a preconscious processor. With PhotoReading you can process written information at rates exceeding a page a second. This is really not a radical idea. The concepts used in the design of PhotoReading have been around for centuries. One major breakthrough in the development of the PhotoReading whole mind system is how you gaze at a page of text. What we developed is a visual state to ensure that when you look at written information, it goes directly to the vast memory stores of the inner mind.

PhotoFocus, as we call it, enables you to take in the entire page at once, rather than hard focusing on individual words and word groups. With PhotoFocus you bypass the limitations of the conscious mind to gain direct access to the unlimited processing potential of the brain. The essence of PhotoFocus involves "seeing with soft eyes." This contrasts with hard focus, which is our normal practice of getting a sharp, clear image of a single word, phrase, or line of print. With PhotoFocus we open up our peripheral vision and mentally photograph entire pages.

You will learn more about the PhotoReading whole mind system in Chapter 10. Right now, you can play with PhotoFocus in the exercise that follows. Aim to experience a visual phenomenon PhotoReaders call the "cocktail weenie effect."

To see the cocktail weenie effect, look at a spot on the wall opposite you. Now, while continuing to look at the spot, hold your hands about 18 inches in front of your eyes. Then bring the tips of your index fingers together.

As you gaze at the spot just above the top of your index fingers, notice in your visual field what is happening to your index fingers. Keep your eyes relaxed and do not worry about bringing anything into sharp focus.

You will notice a ghost image that looks like a third finger or a little party sausage.

Seeing the cocktail weenie demonstrates that you are diverging your eyes instead of converging them on a fixed point of hard focus. When you diverge your focus, you soften your visual field and expand your peripheral awareness. You can see the effect only when you do not look directly at your fingers.

You can apply the same effect to the pages of a book. Fix your gaze on a point comfortably beyond the top of the book or at a spot on the wall, while noticing in your peripheral vision the four edges of the book and the white space between the paragraphs. Because your eyes are diverging, you will see a double crease between the left-hand and right-hand pages. Begin to notice a little rounded strip of a phantom page between the crease lines. That is what we call the "blip page."

You can learn more about PhotoFocus in my book *PhotoReading*. For now, consider that PhotoFocus gives you a direct visual channel to your inner mind. When you use this gaze to zip through books, you will recognize the fabulous assistance your inner mind offers.

PhotoFocus can be thought of as a kind of "second sight." As a neurological phenomenon, it can be used in other ways to open your visual sensory systems and increase your ability to notice more useful information in your world.

Nelson Zink, at the Embudo Center in New Mexico, gives seminars on "Nightwalking." This process allows you to walk outside in total darkness, on moonless nights, using a technique that is the PhotoFocus corollary. When PhotoReading, we use second sight to gather information from the pages of text while we gaze at a distant point. When nightwalking, we use second sight to gather information from the terrain by holding our gaze at a point eighteen inches in front of our eyes and by staring at the end of a rod attached to the visor of a baseball cap.

Does nightwalking work? It is remarkable! I have led groups on wooded trails for miles. They do not stumble on uneven ground or lose the trail. One man ducked for no reason that he could consciously figure out, but, when he reached overhead, he realized his inner mind had warned him of a low branch projecting from a tree at forehead level.

Second sight is a useful tool in developing Step 2 of Natural Brilliance. Viewing the world with soft eyes is a common training technique in the martial arts. For example, a master of Aikido who can defend himself against ten attackers approaching simultaneously has developed 360-degree awareness. I have found writings that suggest a connection between this soft gaze and an ancient Tibetan tradition known as "Splitting the Ethers." Also, Carlos Castenada described a similar open visual gaze in *The Teachings of Don Juan: A Yaqui Way of Knowledge* and in his other books about his Southwest Indian warrior/teacher Don Juan.

Those of us who live in a typical modern lifestyle can practice opening our visual senses in our everyday situations. You can instantly begin to notice useful information all around you. Here's how:

When you are driving in a car, aim high. Move your gaze toward a point on the horizon. Simultaneously notice information coming from your rearview mirror and from your sideview mirrors. Through your peripheral vision, also notice information from the sides of the road.

When walking, practice the same gaze. Imagine an arc stretched from your forehead to the horizon. Let your gaze contain the arc plus the people and objects immediately around you. One woman reported that, when walking through the skyway system in downtown Minneapolis, she was aware that the woman directly behind her was wearing a red dress. When she turned around to look, she was right. No doubt, her mind had picked up reflected information around her.

Use the same techniques when walking through large crowds. Rather than looking directly at people, go into soft focus to determine your path. The same concept is used when PhotoReading a newspaper or magazine. Rather than focusing on individual articles, pass through such materials in PhotoFocus, letting your inner mind process everything. Then your mind can show you the ideal path to obtain the information you need, taking you to specific articles and paragraphs.

All of these techniques will help to open, strengthen, and balance your visual system, allowing it to serve you fully. You will notice more useful information and build a database that will help you respond more effectively to the world around you.

Enhance Your Auditory Sense

Similar to noticing useful information visually, you also can improve the quality of your auditory sense. In truth, we are all hearing only a part of the total auditory spectrum.

If you had your ears tested, you would see an audiogram of what frequencies you can consciously hear. Dr. Alfred Tomatis, a French audiologist, wrote *The Conscious Ear*, translated in English by sound expert Don Campbell. Dr. Tomatis explains that we tend to hear only the sounds our native culture and language habituate us to hear and respond to.

People from India do not make the *F* sound. To pronounce it is difficult, largely because they do not hear it. In Mandarin Chinese there are four intonations used in pronouncing words. Depending on the way it is said, the sound *MA* has four completely different meanings.

Learning another language offers a perfect opportunity to broaden your audiogram. My colleague Peter Kline used a great technique to help Susan, a woman from the South, say the word *oil*. The only way she could pronounce it was *Earl*. Here is what he did.

Peter played a recorded selection of classical music, which offers the brain a wide audio spectrum, and turned on an audio recorder. Then he told Susan to repeat after him:

Peter: Oil
Susan: Earl
Peter: Oil
Susan: Earl
Peter: Oil
Susan: Eril
Peter: Oil
Susan: Eryll
Peter: Oil
Susan: Oy-ill
Peter: Oil
Susan: Oil

Throughout the experiment, Susan *could not consciously perceive* any difference in the way she pronounced the word *oil*. After the experiment, Peter played her recorded voice back to her. To her amazement, she heard herself say the word correctly. Only then did Susan realize it was within her capacity to extend her aural range.

Although Susan reverted to saying *Earl* when Peter turned off the classical music, with further play, she began to hear and speak differently.

The unconscious acquisition of language is demonstrated when an expatriate lives in the United States for a few years. An Englishman I know speaks, to my ear, with a clearly discernible British accent. However, when he returns home, his family chides his "dreadful" American accent. I only detect it in his pronunciation of certain words; his high-toned *kahn* has flattened out to a plain Midwestern *can*.

A powerful story of the nonconscious acquisition of information came from Tom, a Boston PhotoReader who worked for Volvo. To practice PhotoReading and prepare for a business trip to Sweden, Tom PhotoRead the Swedish-English dictionary several dozen times. Only PhotoReading it for a few minutes each time, he never spoke a word of the language.

When he arrived, his host took him to dinner at a local restaurant. After he ordered, his host said, "I didn't know you spoke Swedish."

"I don't," replied Tom, perplexed at the man's statement.

"Come on, you're joking. You just ordered your meal in flawless Swedish!"

"No," Tom shook his head.

"But you did," the man laughed. To prove it, he called the waitress back to the table. "Did my friend just order his meal in Swedish?" he asked the waitress.

"Yes," she replied. "Beautiful Swedish," she added.

Tom's stunned response was, "What did I order?"

When she told him, Tom quipped, "Well, that's exactly what I wanted!"

While Tom was in Sweden, his brain heard the audiogram characteristic of that culture. In effect, the restaurant served as an auditory smörgasbord. Spontaneously and unconsciously his brain had activated the language. From that point on, Tom was able to make sense of what was being said when people spoke Swedish around him at business meetings. He did not speak the language again on his trip, but he understood—at an intuitive level.

Besides listening to classical music and PhotoReading in foreign languages before travel, you can enhance your auditory perception in other ways. I also encourage you to open your ear to your inner world. Quieting the conscious mind and gently refocusing attention increases control of your inner mind:

First, quiet the world around you. Practice driving without turning on the radio or sound system, or sit contemplatively in a quiet surrounding. Listen to your own mind. Ask yourself a question and notice what happens. With purposeful listening, find the "still, small voice within," the voice of your higher intelligence. The ancient concept: *Ask and it shall be given unto you*, connects you to the source of infinite intelligence.

Second, quiet the mind. Occasionally, after a busy, anxious day, we hear mindless audio loops playing. You have probably repeated a tune or run a movie scene in your head over and over. You can interrupt the audio loop by inserting a replacement. For example, I substitute a chant I learned in meditation classes. Or, I sing a favorite hymn several times. Sometimes I choose to remember a pleasant memory or anticipate a positive future event. Any of those chosen thoughts supplants mindless loops and gives me authority over my thinking process once again.

Enhance Your Feeling Sense

Have you ever said "I feel down" or "I feel up today"? These statements refer to the movement of energy in your body. When you feel stuck, your body is alerting you that it has responded to your stress by allocating energy for fight or flight. During this alert, you cannot gain access to your other inner resources.

Try the following experiment:

> Stand up for a moment. Slump your shoulders forward, get a frown on your face, and hang your head. Tilt your pelvis so that your stomach goes in and your knees go out. Now think to yourself in a depressed-sounding inner voice, "Gosh, I feel wonderful! This is the best day of my life!"

How did that feel? Ridiculous, right?

> Now try this: Straighten your back and legs. Stand straight with your shoulders back and relaxed, your head tilted so that your face looks slightly up. Let a subtle smile grace the corners of your mouth and your eyes. Flex your knees slightly so that you feel springy in your legs. Now think to yourself in an upbeat, excited voice, "I feel totally awful; this is the worst day of my life!"

How did that feel? Isn't it strange to have your body and inner voice working in opposition to your affirmation? This experiment shows how profoundly your physiology and self-talk influence your feelings. The way you operate in the world depends on how you feel. If you want to notice what is happening in your world, assume the physiology that makes you most receptive to information around and in you.

Barbara Brenan, author of *Hands of Light*, describes a process of developing "High Sense Perception," with which a person can perceive the energy fields around and inside living organisms. According to Brenan, noticing subtle energies allows for self-healing, self-transformation, and healing others.

You can feel your own subtle energies with a little patience and persistence. Notice them as you quiet your body and mind. I use the exercise discipline known as hatha yoga.

Some people may imagine a yogi to be a 90-pound turbaned East Indian swami, turning himself into a pretzel. Though I do not look like that, I continue to practice yoga as a path to spinal strength, physical flexibility, and mental control. Since teaching hatha yoga in college, I have practiced it off and on throughout my adult life.

The goal of many Eastern traditions is to strengthen the nervous system. They begin with the concept that all energy originates in the "Qi" center—equivalent to the solar plexus—and all movement arises from the spine. Hatha builds strength, balance, and awareness in both the solar plexus and the spine. By practicing a few simple exercises and postures each day, I enjoy increased energy and ease. Before teaching a course or giving a speech, I make a point to spend a few minutes doing my favorite hatha routine.

You can count on the fact that as you gain strength, balance, and awareness in your physical body, you will simultaneously increase the information your physical senses offer you. The goal of Step 2, Notice, is to increase your sensory acuity.

I have studied another system, called *Edu-K* or *Educational Kinesiology*, which provides incredible benefit to any learner. Developed by Dr. Paul Dennison and his wife, Gail, Edu-K offers easy exercises for balancing the body and mind for effective learning.

Think of physical balance in three dimensions. You can balance vertically—up and down; laterally—left and right; as well as horizontally—forward and back. The techniques of Edu-K are described in a brief easy-to-follow way in the Dennisons' book *Brain Gym: Simple Activities for Whole Brain Learning*. You can do one exercise right now if you would like.

> Stand up. March in place, raising your knees alternately to waist level. Touch your knees with opposite hands: left hand to right knee, right hand to left knee. The Dennisons call this *the cross-crawl* pattern; they maintain it strengthens lateral balance. You may also find it energizes you. I recommend the cross-crawl whenever you have been sitting for more than twenty minutes. Dr. Dennison's contributions break through traditional views of learning by demonstrating the human nervous system does

not learn effectively when it is out-of-balance. When we get too far out-of-balance, we "switch off."

Other simple ways to "switch on" and enhance your Natural Brilliance are found in Christine Ward and Jan Daley's excellent book *Learning to Learn: Strategies for Accelerating Learning and Boosting Performance.* These New Zealand teachers suggest:

- Drink water
- Fill your lungs with fresh air
- Do basic brain gym exercises
- Do aerobic exercise
- Do relaxation or meditation exercises

In addition the authors recommend proper sleep and diet, pleasing colors, natural lighting, good odors, slow music, and natural fibers in clothing and furnishings.

Which ones particularly appeal to you? Use those to enhance your personal and professional development.

Increase Your Intuitive Capacities

Are you psychic? You suspected I was going to ask that, didn't you? Over the years of teaching thousands of people how to use their intuition, I have concluded that we are all born with remarkable perceptual abilities. These abilities, if developed into skills, would be called "psychic" by anyone who did not know better.

Increasing your awareness of internal sensory representations can actually develop your intuition and extrasensory perception (ESP), because your internal pictures, sounds, and feelings have important connections to conscious and nonconscious sensory perceptions. Intuition is commonly thought of as knowledge without prior sensory perception. My redefinition of intuition is knowledge without prior *conscious* sensory perception. We can rely on our nonconscious processes to deliver us the equivalent of "psychically intuitive" abilities. And, we can have it just for the asking.

During a recent PhotoReading class in Mexico, an engineer asked me how he could develop his intuition. Guilliermo feared that, as an analytical thinker, he was without intuition of any kind. I told him, "We can play a little game. I will say the name *John* three times, each time thinking of a different person. I will mix the order, but I will tell you now that one will be my son, one a friend, and one my father-in-law."

Guilliermo was correct in every guess. He said he could sense my father-in-law in a different way, so I asked him to describe John Blackford to me. He described my father-in-law with uncanny accuracy. He intuited that John had been in the Navy and the ministry. He concluded with the fact that John's hair was black, although mostly gone on top. All true.

"I had no idea I could do this," he said with a mixture of astonishment and glee.

If you never experiment, how can you discover your abilities? Everyone has a capacity of genius; it is up to each of us to let his or her genius come alive.

I encourage you to play with your intuition. Think of anything you choose, and ask yourself questions about it. Asking questions develops your internal sensory awareness. Think of a time when you had a strong intuition that turned out to be correct. Even the best psychics have a hit ratio of only 80 percent. So consider anything over 50 percent better than chance and excellent.

Consider how that intuition came to you. Did a picture, a voice, or a feeling part of your intuition reach your conscious mind? Ask yourself to remember the signal that occurred just before you became aware of the sensory perception. Was it a feeling, a voice, or a picture? The seat of your intuition is the awareness that lies at the periphery of your consciousness.

For many people in the American culture, the kinesthetic, or felt sense, is the place where our intuition resides; at the same time we are most out of touch with our feelings. We tend to describe our "out of conscious" sense as "mysterious." For Americans, the visual and auditory senses are the most frequently used and the least mysterious. To get in touch with your own mysterious source of information, your intuition, explore.

Explore everything mentioned so far in your intuition, your least favored senses, the periphery of your awareness, the limits of your sensory awareness, and the distinctions you can make around and within you at any moment in time. Be curious about and receptive to what you discover.

Summary

Step 2, Notice, can feel a lot like playing. Take a curious, open minded approach when you feel stuck. A playful approach switches on the whole mind. I define genius as the product of a mind fully in use. Explore the suggestions in this chapter to notice how easily you can get past being stuck to switch on your genius.

Step 1 and Step 2 together—Release and Notice—create a state of relaxed awareness. When you have achieved this state, you are prepared for the activation of Step 3, Respond. You can realize the full power of your potential when you move in the direction of your desires. Whether you take a step of action or not, whether you fail or succeed, your personal power and genius shine as you respond.

Consider using one or more of the suggestions from this chapter each day until you have experienced all of them. Put a check mark in the box to indicate your progress.

Action Checklist for Notice

- ❑ Noticing Break: Notice what you are not noticing. Check in at various intervals during the day. Notice what you are not paying attention to. What kinesthetic, auditory, and visual information impinged on your senses that caused you to switch off?
- ❑ Soft Gaze: Use the concept of PhotoFocus to softly gaze at the world around you. Expand your peripheral vision to take in everything around you at once without focusing on any one thing.
- ❑ Listen Within: Choose quiet surroundings. Quiet the buzzing mind chatter that may dominate your thinking. Listen to your own still, small voice.
- ❑ Stretch: Do some simple yoga postures or Tai Chi movements to enhance your energy flow and balance.
- ❑ Edu-K Cross Crawl: Do the cross crawl pattern for a minute after sitting for more than twenty minutes. Also switch on by drinking water and breathing fresh air.
- ❑ Develop Intuition: Ask yourself a question to notice the visual, auditory, and kinesthetic information that comes to you. Make guesses based on your internal sensory perceptions and check them out with others.

Respond

Step 3: Respond involves taking action in order to assess the value of what changes. Everything we do and do not do influences the results we get in life. Although we want to make things turn out well, paradoxically, sometimes our actions make things worse.

This chapter examines making decisions and taking actions that lead to quantum leaps in performance. Recognizing how we create oscillation and what we can do to minimize or dampen oscillation is only part of the story. The step of Respond in the Natural Brilliance model is the point of departure from stuck state to genius.

Marcus Wynne is a former government agent, a special weapons and tactics (S.W.A.T.) expert, highly trained in counterterrorist techniques. He enrolled in one of my courses on hypnosis to enhance his skills and understanding of human behavior.

He questioned what I told everyone in the course within thirty minutes of gathering. "You are all going to do a complete session of hypnosis with a partner."

"This can't be," he thought. "Nobody in here knows anything about hypnosis. What about all the safety issues?"

Marcus appreciated the success everyone experienced during that opening exercise. Throughout the weekend the high level of skill he obtained was beyond his expectations. Rather than delivering a heady lecture on hypnosis, I aimed to facilitate the participants in one weekend of practitioner training to do remarkably skilled changework. As a final exam, they performed medical hypnosis under the watchful eye of a physician. Each of them guided their subjects to control pain and bleeding. During the test, the hypnotist slipped the physician's hypodermic needle through the skin of the subject's hand without discomfort to the subject.

After graduating from the course, Marcus began looking at the training methods in his own field. He quickly understood the deficiencies of most traditional training methods. In Marcus's words:

"What I realized is that one of the big differences between Paul Scheele's training programs and most other programs is that Paul assumes people are bright enough to do a good job. Rather than spending time teaching unnecessary rules and installing the fear of failure, he starts with the most difficult task first, and they just do it.

"It didn't surprise me one bit to see that typical handgun training and civilian combat scenario training for law enforcement officers do everything wrong. The trainers spend an incredible amount of time telling people what *not* to do."

Marcus designed a different course. The final exam came only four hours after the course started. A young woman who had never held a handgun was put to the test next to a five-year veteran law enforcement agent who had not taken Marcus's course. In four years of prior military service, this man had received hundreds of thousands of dollars worth of combat training, including S.W.A.T. courses. The only time the woman had ever seen a gun was once, three years earlier.

In the test an "assailant" attacked each of the participants individually. Their job was to defend themselves by drawing their weapons, a .38-caliber revolver, and firing blanks (with cotton wading) at the chest of the attacker.

The man drew his weapon and fired six times—in rapid succession—all around the attacker. Never once did he score a stopping shot. The woman confidently pumped all six rounds in a tight cluster into the attacker's chest.

Marcus Wynne continued to refine his training techniques. Now his work receives international acclaim for its effectiveness in achieving critical skills retention under life-threatening stress.

Head in the Right Direction: It's Not What You Don't Want

What is the Natural Brilliance difference that made the big difference? What in Marcus Wynne's approach leads to quantum leaps in performance? When you understand this next point, you will have the essence of Natural Brilliance.

Let's go back the nature of stuck states. When people are stuck, they are expending most of their energy oscillating between opposing actions, both of which contain negative consequences. They ask themselves, "What are all the things I don't want?"

When asked a powerful question, the mind tends to go on a search to answer it. It immediately generates an enormous list of previous learning experiences. Marcus realized that those previous experiences were saying "Here is what you don't want." For example: *Don't harm anyone unintentionally. Don't point the gun in the wrong direction. Be extremely careful to ensure everyone's safety. Never carry a loaded handgun unless the safety is on. Never fire your weapon unless you are absolutely sure that you can live with the consequences of your action.* With all those contradictory messages, no wonder oscillation occurred every time a law enforcement officer had to fire a gun in the line of duty.

Our life experience teaches us that when we do something and don't get what we want, we should stop and do the opposite. But doing the opposite can be a prescription for oscillation. What we need is the question "What do I want?" The young woman in the handgun training clearly wanted to defend herself. The law enforcement agent next to her was filled with *don'ts* that kept him unconsciously oscillating between doing the task and *not* doing the task *incorrectly*.

What is it you want? It may seem ridiculous, but that crucial question is rarely asked in traditional psychotherapy. Even more dramatic is how few therapy clients can answer the question. The reason? They are completely oriented to their problems, not to their outcomes. They suffer from their problems, they discuss their problems, they get insight about their problems, but they spend little time clearly articulating what they want instead of their problems. Until we decide on our outcomes and respond to achieve them, we cannot fully discover our Natural Brilliance.

Natural Brilliance does something quite simple. It trains your brain to ask a very different question—the outcome question—"What do I want?" When your mind goes on an immediate search for the answer to this question, it creates possibilities, choices, options. The clearer you are about what you want, the more easily your mind can achieve it.

The third step in the Natural Brilliance model—Respond—pops us out of stuck states by eliciting a powerful answer to What do I want?

Step 3 naturally overcomes the limitations of previous ineffective training.

You may have heard the statement, "If you always do what you've always done, you'll always get what you've always gotten." The message is if you want to get something new, you must do something different. Responding means decisively taking appropriate action in the direction of your desired goal.

Find Balance in Oscillation: Juggle

Learning to juggle requires movement, balance, and a willingness to fail. My belief is that anything worth doing is worth doing badly at first. Juggling teaches you that perfectionism does not work. No one juggles well at the beginning.

When you juggle, you must perform only two actions. You must toss the ball in an arc from one hand to the other, and you must catch the ball you throw. Juggling becomes difficult because you must perform these actions simultaneously—with at least three balls.

For most people, juggling is a confusing blur of oscillating movement. Anyone who casually attempts juggling usually ends up declaring, "I can't do this!" Most people confronting their stuck states say the same thing. They perceive a confusing blur of competing responses, which leave them convinced there is no hope.

Lessons from the Art of Juggling by Michael J. Gelb and Tony Buzan explains the connection between juggling and experiential learning. I had decided after years of repeated attempts that I was "juggling-disabled." One evening I attended a rousing performance by the Flying Karamozov Brothers. Afterward, they offered to coach members of the audience in their art. Their simple teaching method encouraged mastery of throwing and catching one ball at a time. When I could do one ball well, they graduated me to two balls. When I could do two balls, I graduated to three. Every time I dropped a ball, I picked it up without self-depreciation and took it from where I left off. I learned how to juggle in less than ten minutes.

Responding, like juggling, requires finding a place of balance inside an oscillation. For many of us, balancing is easier said than done. Most adults try to learn something with ineffective strategies they used in school, such as "get it the first time with 100-percent accuracy."

Would you believe this about adult learners: Although it takes performing up to fifty trials before adults can accurately judge that they cannot develop a particular ability, most people usually quit within the first ten times of doing something unsuccessfully?

Imagine if infants had the same learning style as adults while attempting to learn how to walk. After landing face first in the dirt the tenth time, they would roll over and say, "Sorry, Mom, I can't walk. Looks like I'm going to be a crawler for the rest of my life. Just because you're a genius at walking, doesn't mean I can be. I've tried and failed. I just can't get it to happen."

Respond is characterized by persistence. You must hold the belief *you can do it* to such an extent that giving up is not even an option. Your will to succeed will find the way to succeed.

Confront Your Fears—The Power Appears

Motivation expert Dennis Waitley suggests two typical approaches to life. One is *goal achieving*; the other *stress relieving*. If strong fear and weak motivation come together, stress relieving is our likely path. It makes sense considering that when we hit an internal stop sign, we tend to do a quick U-turn for fear we might get whacked.

How can people reasonably confront their fears when every internal urge screams "Flee!" Fortunately, you come fully equipped with a vast source of personal strength. Strength to respond results from setting clear outcomes with clear motives or purpose, and connecting to internal resources. Here is how:

1) Using the Natural Brilliance model, approach goal achieving with relaxed alertness, feeling internally balanced and clear about the many choices and options available to you. When you take action, you quickly recognize if your response moves you away from what you desire. By performing a trial and noticing the feedback, you can get a clear sense of what it takes for you to succeed. *Trial and feedback* enhances your decision-making, and increases your motivation as well. Fear cannot restrain a powerful intention.

2) Being physically and emotionally present in the face of fear allows you to remain resourceful. As a result of Step 1, Release, you are physically and emotionally relaxed and present. As a result of Step 2, Notice, you

are mentally alert and connected to your current sensory perceptions, both internal and external. Relaxed alertness creates a connection to the wisdom of your nonconscious mind. When you consciously respond to events in your life from a place of resourcefulness, you will effectively achieve outcomes.

Our nonconscious mind controls our habitual behaviors. When we respond with fear, the nonconscious is simply doing its best to protect us.

You can easily train your nonconscious to move you past fears. In fact an instant ignition switch in your nonconscious turns on the total power of body-mind. "Just Do It!" is the theme of the successful Nike campaign. It emphasizes that 99 percent of the work to overcome your fears happens when you show up and go for your dreams.

Writer-philosopher Ralph Waldo Emerson put it this way: "He who does not the thing has not the power. He who does the thing has the power." When we respond with purpose to attain our goals, the nonconscious delivers the required strength. Simply engage yourself enough to respond, and all else follows. Your mind and body can generate enough power to overcome your fear.

Fire Up the Heat of Passionate Desire

You must be willing to fail in order to win. If you cannot stand the prospect of losing, you forfeit the game. Harry S. Truman declared: "If you can't stand the heat, get out of the kitchen!" Eliminating the fear of failure is the same as eliminating any other fear. To respond and achieve your desires, you must show up to play in the game, not run away or hide. Not only must you stand resolute in the heat of the kitchen, you must fire up an even greater heat of passionate desire for the life you want to create.

Most people are blinded by their goals. By their own internal measures, they judge themselves a success or a failure. But failure cannot happen to you; you do it to yourself. When you miss the mark, you can choose to call what you got *feedback*. You fail only when you give up believing in yourself. There is no other failure in the world.

Dr. Paul Watzlawick and the Palo Alto Brief Therapy Clinic in California developed a breakthrough strategy for lifelong learning that makes subsequent goal achievement surprisingly simple.

Although your actions may not always accomplish your goals, they always produce an outcome. If you know how to accept what your actions produce, you can use every outcome you produce to guide you toward your goal. "Whatever course of action you take," says Dr. Watzlawick, "I am going to ask that you report any small concrete indicator of success, any movement in the direction of your goal."

When you witness the effects of your actions, you open yourself to perceiving progress toward and away from your goals. Consequently the only feedback is "I have not arrived yet."

The brief therapy breakthrough changes our orientation. As we respond and witness the effects, we recognize movement. We experience success *in the direction* of our goals without having to achieve the goal just yet. When we take the pressure off ourselves, we maintain our balance, enjoy the journey, and keep learning all the time.

Earl Nightingale, the self-improvement herald from the 1950s through the 80s, made famous the line "Success is the progressive realization of a worthy ideal." That quote sums up the purpose of the step of Respond

Respond with Natural Brilliance

Let's summarize Step 3 of the Natural Brilliance model.

- By responding we seek a balance point within an oscillating system.
- Responding effectively requires an outcome orientation and decisions that are based on knowing the desired results you want to produce.
- Resourcefulness happens when you are relaxed and alert. Relaxed means physically and emotionally present; alert means your sensory systems are online.
- You realize most of your personal power when you show up, engage, and do what you desire to accomplish.
- The best learning occurs when you make concrete, incremental changes in the direction of your goal.
- If you value and integrate the feedback from your actions, all outcomes you produce can lead to learning.
- Persistence is crucial. Discipline and hard work are rarely as important as persistent actions based on informed choice and learning about what works.

We can accomplish a big shift in results from a small shift in orientation. In a relatively new field of mathematics dubbed *fuzzy logic*, big results are being achieved by looking at systems in terms of successive approximations of correctness. Fuzzy logic described in the book, *Fuzzy Thinking: The New Science of Fuzzy Logic* by Bart Kosko and Tony Buzan, departs from typical true/false, either/or, black/white kinds of thinking. That type of thinking and language creates oscillation. Rather, it uses both/and, inclusive, integrative, gray-tone language characteristic of Natural Brilliance.

In the short time it has been used, fuzzy logic has spawned a multibillion-dollar industry using computers to control machines. For example, elevators and air conditioners are no longer "on" or "off," but "kind of on" or "sort of off." Now, we can make machines continually respond to feedback, which creates successive approximations leading to a goal.

Imagine, a machine with the benefit of a "continuous improvement" approach to problem-solving. It gets smarter with every action it takes. Well, guess what? You are infinitely more capable of learning than any machine we can ever produce. As a matter of fact, the mathematicians who developed fuzzy logic and inventors who designed those machines used human capabilities as their model. Your body and brain succeed on the same principles as fuzzy logic and continuous improvement.

Summary

I encourage you to always celebrate every inch of your progress, as well as your accomplishments. You can achieve whatever you set your mind on. You can gain access to energy reserves you might never before have thought possible. Taking time to acknowledge and reinforce your experiences of success is Step 4 of the Natural Brilliance model: Witness.

Consider using one or more of the suggestions from this chapter each day until you have experienced all of them. Put a check mark in the box to indicate your progress.

Action Checklist for Respond

❑ Establish Clear Outcomes: Write down the results you want to produce. Do your best to ensure your goal is achievable, believable, measurable, testable, and worthwhile.

❑ Get into State: For optimum resourcefulness, enter a state of relaxed alertness before performing an important activity.

❑ Show Up: Determine to do something you have been avoiding, and show up ready to go. Discover what happens when you start a task you had put off in the past.

❑ Measure Your Progress: Recognize any small concrete changes in the direction of your goal. Celebrate any and all progress you make.

❑ Go Easy on Yourself: There is no failure, only learning. Take time to review whatever outcomes you produce, then value and integrate the feedback from your actions.

❑ Stay on It: Keep choosing and responding, far past the point where you would have quit before. Give new behaviors at least fifty trials. Keep learning about what works.

> I grew up being told that if a thing is worth doing, it's worth doing well. Now I know that doing something well is easy if you know how. It's learning to do it well that's so hard. I recognize that if a thing is worth doing it's worth doing badly. That's the only way you'll ever be able to learn it. I'm an expert at doing things badly so I'll be able eventually to do them well.
>
> **Peter Kline, Chairman of the Board**
> **Integra Learning Systems**

> "So what's the challenge in the first simulation?" asked Elan. "Resignation and hopelessness," answered the elder. "Many people set out with a goal in life. But when it becomes hazy or adversity sets in, they often succumb. These people let circumstances dictate their lives, never realizing that they have the power to change things." Elan knew he couldn't hesitate. "I'd like to do it," he said. "I'd like to realize my power to confront and change things."
>
> **D. Trinidad Hunt**

> You may have heard a joke about the definition of insanity. Insanity is doing the same things and expecting different results.

7

Witness

Imagine the safety and permission you would have for learning if you could honestly affirm that whatever experience you have is okay. If this safety is not available to you intellectually, emotionally, and physically, you might oscillate away from your goal and enter a stuck state. Witness, the remarkable safe oasis of self observation, nurtures us and keeps us oriented to manifesting our highest potential in life.

When my wife, Libby, was a little girl, she desperately wanted to jump off the high dive. The high dive at the beach where her family vacationed one summer stood as the centerpiece of fun. Every day she watched her brother, sister, and cousin performing crazy jumps from the high board and splashing into the waves. Although Libby longed to dive, she was terrified of the height.

On the last afternoon of vacation, she was determined. She scaled the ladder, but once on top, she quickly sat on the platform and clung to the rail. Her siblings tried everything to get her going. At first they encouraged and enticed her. Then they goaded her. When that didn't work, they cajoled her. Finally, they even tried to push her—to no avail. The more they urged, the tighter she gripped. In the meantime, all the kids lined up on the ladder had to scramble over her to execute their own cannonballs and swan dives.

Later, when the time came for her family to leave the beach, with everyone else on shore, Libby knew no one would bother her. She stood alone, edged to the end of the board, and looked over. In her mind she saw herself jumping and surviving. She held her nose, closed her eyes, and leaped.

She loved it! She quickly paddled back to the diving platform. After doing "just one more dive" six times, her frustrated family finally dragged little Libby back to shore.

In the Natural Brilliance retreat, I demonstrate exactly how Libby took her leap of faith off the diving platform and what she learned in the process. Professional hypnotists call what she did the "falling backwards test," and the same exercise has also made the rounds in personal development courses as the "trust fall." Here are the steps:

Stand with your feet together and your arms folded while someone stands behind you with arms extended, palms facing your shoulder blades, legs set shoulder width apart, one foot ahead of the other. When you close your eyes and lean back, the "catcher" will stop your fall with waiting hands.

For some, falling is difficult. If they have fear, they will try to catch themselves mid-fall by putting one foot behind them. However, those who do accomplish the trust fall follow a similar strategy every time. They see themselves landing in the catcher's hands and feeling safe.

So, in your mind's eye, from a perspective of standing either behind yourself or to the side of yourself, watch your own fall and see the safe catch.

Interestingly, two kinesthetic experiences complement the visual experience. First, as you watch the imaginary self fall and get caught, feel the placement of the catcher's hands on your own back. Second, enjoy a corresponding internal feeling of safety.

The final component is an auditory statement that signals go-ahead. You may hear a voice saying "Okay" or "Let's go!" The words are less important than how the internal voice sounds, not tense and anxious but relaxed and powerful, congruent with the feeling of safety.

Once again the strategy is:

1) Visualize the fall from an observer perspective.
2) Feel the imagined moment of being caught.
3) Feel safe at a gut level.
4) Hear your internal supportive voice give the go-ahead.

The trust fall lies at the heart of witness. When people can witness their own responses to the world, before, during, and after taking action, they can break through to learning.

What would you think if I summarized breakthrough as being a change in your belief in yourself? Most often, you have changed beliefs about your capability when you learned how to choose new behaviors and win. Winning demonstrates capability. But first, you must identify yourself as someone who can win.

Can you recognize that you are in the driver's seat during the witness mode of the learning process? You direct your learning almost exclusively from inside you. Just as little Libby could not be cajoled into jumping from the high dive, you and I are in charge of confronting our own fears and stepping up to challenges that face us. Similarly, we cannot bully ourselves to change. Witness provides safety and freedom for learning and winning. Witness creates a safe place inside to imagine ourselves as winners.

Take a Consultant's Perspective

When I consult with companies, I have the advantage of an outside perspective. I can see things from alongside or behind the scenes, a view most "insiders" do not have as long as they cling to their own problems. Part of my mandate is to facilitate the employees to witness their own process and their own solutions.

Again, when I work with individual clients, I have perspective to view their situations from alongside. I may get an insight they cannot see from their own point of view. But the paradox is that no matter how many great ideas I come up with, the clients themselves must shift their own behavior.

You get to jump off your own high dive.

The objective of Witness in the Natural Brilliance model is to facilitate you in developing your own consultant's point of view. Beyond the stop sign stretches a splendid panorama of choices. From the distance of a consultant's perspective, you can learn efficiently from your own mistakes and successes. Because you are in charge of your own life, learning from the consequences of your own actions reinforces your power as a self-governing individual.

Throughout history, people have placed great value on the insights of wise consultants. Now we call these people *mentor, sage,* or *guru.* In ancient times we knew them as *prophet, oracle,* or *angel.* They have played an enormously important role in the history of human psychic, emotional, and spiritual development. These wise counselors and teachers have always facilitated the unfolding of human potential. In fact, they have guided the evolution of consciousness throughout the ages.

Today our consciousness has evolved to the point where we stand ready to take the next step of human development. Physicist and author Peter Russel, in his book *The White Hole in Time*, suggests humanity's next flight up is "Involution," a supernova of consciousness equivalent to the imploding supernova of a mature star.

In his book Russel offers the following parable:

A mind attached to its beliefs is like a person clinging to a piece of rope.

He holds on for dear life, knowing that if he were to let go he would fall to his death. His parents, his teachers, and many others have told him this is so; and, when he looks around, he can see everyone else doing the same.

Nothing would induce him to let go.

Along comes a wise person. She knows that holding on is unnecessary, that the security it offers is illusory and only holds him where he is. So she looks for a way to dispel his illusions and help him to be free.

She talks of real security, of deeper joy, of true happiness, of peace of mind. She tells him that he can taste this if he will just release one finger from the rope.

"One finger," thinks the man, "that's not too much to risk for a taste of bliss." So he agrees to take this first initiation.

And he does taste greater joy, happiness, and peace of mind.

But not enough to bring lasting fulfillment.

"Even greater joy, happiness, and peace can be yours," she tells him, "if you will just release a second finger."

"This," he tells himself, "is going to be more difficult. Can I do it? Will it be safe? Do I have the courage?" He hesitates, then, flexing his finger, feels how it would be to let go a little more...and takes the risk.

He is relieved to find he does not fall; instead he discovers greater happiness and inner peace.

But could more be possible?

"Trust me," she says. "Have I failed you so far? I know your fears; I know what your mind is telling you—that this is crazy, that it goes against everything you have ever learned—but, please, trust me. Look at me, am I not free? I promise you will be safe, and you will know even greater happiness and contentment.

"Do I really want happiness and inner peace so much," he wonders, "that I am prepared to risk all that I hold dear? In principle, yes; but can I be sure that I will be safe, that I will not fall?" With a little coaxing he begins to look at his fears, to consider their basis, and to explore what it is he really wants. Slowly he feels his fingers soften and relax. He knows he can do it. He knows he must do it. He releases his grip.

As he does so, an even greater sense of peace flows through him.

He is now hanging by one finger. Reason tells him he should have fallen a finger or two ago, but he hasn't. "Is there something wrong with holding on itself?" he asks himself. "Have I been wrong all the time?"

"This one is up to you," she says. "I can help you no further. Just remember that all your fears are groundless."

Trusting his quiet inner voice, he gradually releases the last finger.

And nothing happens.

He stays exactly where he is.

Then he realizes why. He has been standing on the ground all along.

As he looks at the ground, knowing he need never hold on again, he finds true peace of mind.

In that parable, think of the importance of the witness perspective, as in the falling backwards test and Libby's high dive. Witness takes us beyond the limitation of our own beliefs into alternative universes of choice. The final shift in belief is always up to us individually.

Shift Your Perceptual Position

Historically, the term "witness" has been compared to knowledge and testimony. Witness, as I use it, consists of self-knowledge gained from personal experience and knowledge gained from observing the actions of others. This knowledge, gained from the testimony of your senses internally and externally, lets you witness yourself and others with ever-increasing clarity.

Consider three typical perceptual positions from which we experience our world:

"First Person," or the first perceptual position, refers to experiencing life through our own sensory systems. I see my world through my own eyes. I speak in my own voice.

"Second Person," or the second perceptual position, refers to "walking a mile in the other person's shoes" or seeing the world from someone else's point of view. I speak in the second person as I empathize with your position on issues.

"Third Person," or the third perceptual position, refers to perceiving the context in which actions are taking place. I see myself over there, and I see you with me over there, so I mentally position myself as if I were watching the two of us on video. The third perceptual position gets close to the witness perspective I refer to in Step 4 of Natural Brilliance. Close, but not exactly it.

Witness, the fourth perceptual position, takes into account the first, second, and third perceptual positions simultaneously. In it, you can sense Self, Other, and Context with an outcome orientation.

Patricia Danielson, my closest professional colleague in the development of PhotoReading, describes the outcome orientation of witness as a state of "Positive Neutrality." In this state you detach, as an observer, at the same time you believe you and the other person can both achieve your desired results. We distinguish this state from someone trying hard to get a goal—struggling and obsessing over every little failure. Positive neutrality allows us to witness our successes and failures in various situations (or contexts) in a larger life context.

Most cultures have no single word to describe this complex state. Paradoxical in nature, it perceives the existence of opposites and integrates them. From the witness perspective I can say, "My failure today is okay, because I am headed somewhere much more important than this." Witness accepts and resolves duality.

Witness, in its detached involvement, combines the roles of nurturing parent and the consulting observer. Witness takes the meta-position that learning is all there is.

Benefit from Witness

The consequences of responding (Step 3) *without* witnessing (Step 4) can be devastating. When you confront disapproval and punishment in your attempts to learn and to improve the quality of your life, stop signs pop up at every crossroad. Contrary to what some contend, *"constructive* criticism" does not exist. Constructive feedback is far different from the act of finding fault. The judgmental mind criticizes and screams, "Don't do that again!" Fault-finding leads to blame; blame leads to feeling bad about yourself; feeling bad about yourself leads to oscillation. Once the vicious cycle starts, stuck states abound.

When you respond and witness, you can perceive that you did something that did not move you in the direction of your goal. For example, I understood my temper alienated me from the love I wanted to feel with my wife and children. I fully understood my anger at their behaviors was a response based on fear. So what? That is fine. I can continue to blow up in anger until my dying breath. It is my life. No one can change my responses in the world. The question is still "What do I want?" If I want a response other than an angry temper, what would it be?

Notice the oscillation set up by my getting angry and critical of myself for being angry and critical of others? We see a lot of bumper stickers, political cartoons, and wry jokes based on the paradoxes of oscillation. I'm thinking of the person who says "I think prejudiced people should be shot. I hate judgmental people." I remember a lapel button about capital punishment that read: "Why do we kill people who kill people to send a message that killing people is wrong?"

Exposing our shortcomings is not the goal of Witness. The goal is getting what we want. When I fail to achieve what I want, I do not have to hop onto an emotional roller coaster of trying harder only to fail again.

Think of Witness as an oasis experience, a restorative pause in the journey, for the wanderer in the desert. Witness offers perspective in the learning process called life, a pause that touches us emotionally, informs us intellectually, and refreshes us spiritually.

If you have ever gone on a retreat, you may already know the broader benefits of witnessing. In a retreat, you pull back from living life in the external world to get closer to yourself so that you can live fully. The experiences of your life can yield rich information to *inform* you, to *form in* you, and, ultimately, to *form* you. Witness makes this rich source of information available at every level of your being.

Integrate Your Witness in Moments of Truth

Without Witness, it is easy to deny the consequences of my self-defeating and unproductive actions, and thereby lose my *moment of truth*—my chance to learn and grow. When I do something that feels good but does not get me what I want, I face a moment of truth. I know what I have done. But, which perspective will I chose: to learn and be smarter for it or to deny and walk away from it?

For example, I can overspend on a piece of audio gear and rationalize my decision as taking advantage of a good deal. The problem, which I can easily predict from the witness perspective, will come when the "Zero-Interest-for-Six-Months" time period is over. When my short-term buy response compromises my long-range financial goals, I have a moment of truth to face.

As a child I learned that when external authority was not watching, I could get away with things. I could break rules and get at the off-limits goodies of life. As adults, we create rules to govern our behavior and manage ourselves. We create rules because we know *we cannot always follow them*—we cannot *always* live up to our highest expectations. When we break rules, we face consequences. The stronger the rule, the more difficult it is to follow and the greater the consequences.

Witness, however, does not prescribe an automatic consequence. With witness online, you can determine how to respond at the moment of truth from the perspective of a broader life context. Your response coming from the long perspective of witness will more likely benefit your whole life.

Let me offer an analogy: the "near-death" experience of a client in Mexico. Near-death experiences bring us spontaneously into witness. No one knows why, but in the instant of our brush with death, we suddenly review our entire life, seeing it in the broadest of contexts.

My client, Gerardo, put his motorcycle down at high speed in traffic. He plunged under an oncoming pickup truck, only to wake up days later in the hospital. By every calculation, Gerardo should have been killed or permanently disfigured. He healed from the accident completely, unscathed neurologically and physically.

Emotionally, Gerardo had a transformational healing. As he lay in his hospital bed, he began to review his life. Throughout his twenty years of living, people never mattered much to him; he used them as a means to his end. He never gave a second thought to doing others wrong. They were not his problem, but he was certainly their problem.

Gerardo felt that, by some divine intervention, he had been given a second chance in life. He resolved to go to every person he had ever left with ill will and personally apologize to them.

To meet this young man today, you immediately perceive a wisdom beyond his years. Surrounding him is a spiritual radiance and a pure joy for living. His lovely young wife and baby boy are blessings to him of the highest order. Gerardo feels he is doing better the second time around, as a result of what he witnessed about his own life.

You do not have to go to the extreme of a near-death experience in order to witness your life. You can also achieve this special perspective safely and intentionally. Witness allows us to perceive the interconnectedness of our actions to the totality of life. The frightened, fearful person has limited visibility on the outcome of any act. Living life successfully in the long run requires awareness of how responses to life today shape the continuously unfolding future. Your payback for witnessing can be profound.

Think of this present moment on an imaginary timeline that stretches back into the past and forward into the future. It is possible, with the power of your imagination, to witness the course of your life. For example, you can observe the past and witness the path you have traveled. You can also reasonably predict the outcomes you will experience in the future, extending the trajectory of your current habitual behaviors forward in time. Are your behaviors today creating the future you desire? If not, what do you want?

By eliminating fear, which fogs your vision, you will spontaneously generate a big perspective of life. Instead of running up against stop signs, you will get an inner signal to go ahead.

Look into the Shadows

Being clear to witness the context and validity of our actions has strong personal developmental benefits. Witness gives us insight into the repressed, or "shadow," energies we keep hidden from others, plus it exposes the dysfunctional strategies we use to avoid confronting our fears.

Fear imposes a profoundly negating effect on life. Although it is biologically imperative to notice and respond to the warnings that fear signals, fear is seldom good for our well-being. Paradoxically, many times it only gets in our way. Instead of saving our lives, fear often keeps us from living. If we have failed in the past, we respond to fear on the basis of an unconscious faulty conclusion about our capability for the future. Our typical inherently self-defeating responses to fear keep us from tapping our full potential.

If you ever console a child who is afraid of the dark, you will have a chance to observe how we generate mythical fears and cope with them. Children project frightening images beyond the circle of light and generate corresponding tremulous emotions. They conjure up the most hideous monsters lurking deep in the shadows.

One night my youngest son, Scott, woke up cowering from a grotesque monster that lay in wait outside the window near his bed. When I suggested he could consider that the monster had horrible fangs made of marshmallows dripping with hot chocolate sauce, his five-year-old imagination eagerly joined the game. We continued to add red gumdrop eyes, claws of gummy worms, spaghetti hair, and a glorious green frosting hide sparkling with rainbow-colored sprinkles until he fell peacefully back to sleep. Weeks later, he mentioned matter-of-factly that he had seen the monster again. This time, all on his own, he had outfitted him with new features, equally wonderful.

Instead of feeling fear and withdrawing, Scott had been able to feel his insecurity and actively respond. He placed the images and feelings he wanted into the shadows of his mind. Rather than covering his head, he embraced the opportunity.

In the shadows of adults lurk memories of emotionally painful experiences. Most of us bear some wounds. It may be impossible to completely avoid getting hurt while growing up. The big problem with wounding experiences come when we create faulty conclusions about ourselves and generate mythical fears based on them.

For example, the attitude "I'm no good. I can't learn to do anything right" generates mythical fears about failure and success. Such fears cause us to avoid something or to give up learning skills we need. When we witness our choices, we often discover we have chosen to bury part of our aliveness, our creativity, our eagerness to explore life to the fullest.

Robert Bly, poet-laureate of the men's movement in America, wrote in his *A Little Book on the Human Shadow* that we all drag a long bag behind us, stuffed full of the repressed parts of our personality. Often, the bag holds some of our most creative resources, lost to us because of some embarrassing ridicule that hurt enough emotionally. "The nice side of the personality becomes, in our idealistic culture, nicer and nicer," writes Bly. "But the substance in the bag takes on a (regressed) personality of its own...Every part of our personality that we do not love will become hostile to us." These repressed parts are called our *shadow*.

By witnessing your chain of responses to fear, you can create a new path out of the shadows. Perhaps we need nothing more than a dollop of Scott's marshmallows, hot fudge sauce, and rainbow sprinkles. The secret is in replacing fear with love.

Milton R. Cudney, Ph.D., spent thirty years of his professional life researching self-defeating behaviors. His brilliant book with Robert E. Hardy, Ed.D., describes a way out of fear, denial, and self-defeating traps. In their book, *Self-Defeating Behaviors: Free Yourself from the Habits, Compulsions, Feelings, and Attitudes That Hold You Back*, they offer this useful insight:

> Above all, never lose sight of the fact that self-defeating behaviors are both dangerous and deceptive. They come into your life as apparent friends who offer comfort and protection in moments of distress. They help you through these threatening moments, and for this you are grateful—so grateful that you come to believe that you cannot live without their devious company. Sooner or later, though, these behaviors reveal their true nature. At that point, you must face the realization that your self-defeating behaviors have been unworthy companions and untrustworthy guides. The comfort that these behaviors offer is false. If you rely upon them too long, they will lead you away from the road of health, growth, and life. Self-defeating behaviors will, in the end, take you precisely where you didn't want to go.

Manifest Your Highest Good

The exciting opportunity that witness provides goes beyond accomplishing successful results. The Bible refers to the power of integrating the beneficial and detrimental results of our actions. The phrase in 1 John 4:18 "Perfect love casteth out all fear" captures it. William A. Miller, in his book, *Your Golden Shadow*, describes the wealth—gold—to be enjoyed when we reclaim shadow energy.

> We can find a way to bring that negative potential into contact with its counterpart in the persona and effect a unification of these opposites. Thus we find a way to use creatively and constructively what we loathed before or even wanted to deny the existence of within ourselves.

> Furthermore, we discover the unconscious positive elements that are the counterparts of the nastiness in our conscious persona and work to bring about a unification of these opposites.

> Beyond this lies the real gold of all the positive potential within us that never has had the opportunity to see the light of day. What treasures lie hidden in one's unconscious can be discovered only by the one who will seek them out.

In the Natural Brilliance model we progress from Notice to Respond to Witness. In the Witness phase we have the opportunity to integrate everything we learned and prepare for the next step in our evolution by releasing once again. That's right. We cycle back to Release and extend our genius even further toward our goals.

In this continuous cycling we find the pattern of the successful life-long learner. In the cycle of the Natural Brilliance model, the fire in our passion for life is fueled with each step of learning we take. We experience enthusiasm for life and learning simultaneously. Enthusiasm, from the Latin root word *entheos*, meaning "God within," is an ever flowing fountain of hope. The brilliant future we desire to create in our lives manifests each day, with each step of Natural Brilliance we take.

Summary

Consider using one or more of the suggestions from this chapter each day until you have experienced all of them. Put a check mark in the box to indicate your progress.

Action Checklist for Witness

- ❏ Fall Backwards: With a partner, do the falling backwards test. Discover what it has to offer you about knowing it is okay to proceed.
- ❏ Consultant's Perspective: Pretend to sit across from yourself and take on the perspective of a wise and trusted counselor. Have a conversation with the imaginary part of you about a problem you want to resolve. Hold no investment or judgment about the outcome; simply learn from the conversation.
- ❏ Perceptual Position: Remember a difficult situation involving you and another person. Think through what happened from each of the three perceptual positions; first (yours), second (the other person's), third (a disassociated view of the whole context). Finally, witness what you learned by examining all three.
- ❏ Oasis Experience: At night before going to sleep, review your day without judgment or criticism. Offer yourself blessing and celebration for doing your best. Ask yourself "What do I want for my life?" Resolve to implement your intention when you awaken tomorrow.
- ❏ Moment of Truth: Determine to face up to a moment of truth when it arrives today. Confront your self-defeating behavior with the question "What do I want to create for myself right now?" When you can answer the question, thank yourself and immediately take the first step to manifesting your highest good.
- ❏ Peek Into the Shadows: Explore the beliefs you hold that you do not want to admit to yourself. Examine your reactions, whether they be curious attraction or repulsion, to traits in others. Examine your behaviors, looks, dirty jokes you retell, and movies you watch. What taboos do you tend to break or wish you could? What do you do that you consider socially nasty?
- ❏ Shadow Dancing: Find ways to creatively and constructively use your nastiness. One warning: Acknowledge your shadow, but be careful not to indulge it. Set boundaries around exploring your shadow to ensure what you do serves your best interest.

8

Put Natural Brilliance to Work for You

A businessman came to see me for individual consultations. He employed thousands of people and made multimillion-dollar decisions every day. When it came to his personal life, however, he managed very poorly. His marriage had ended in a tumultuous divorce. His dates usually disintegrated into social disasters. He could not even choose a restaurant for dinner. Because he could not decide what decor he liked, he had settled for furnishing the living room of his high-priced condominium with aluminum lawn chairs.

Working with this man taught me an important lesson. Success strategies do not necessarily transfer from one area of a person's life to another. The skill sets used to accomplish business and financial success are completely different from those used to manage personal and close interpersonal issues.

For many reasons in his personal history, this man had realized his genius in business, yet he was stuck in his personal life. In my experience most people seem to enjoy great success in some areas of their lives, while they struggle in other areas.

Think of your successes. In these areas, you have learned and developed the essential skills to produce effective results. In doing so, you have cycled through the four steps of Natural Brilliance many times. Through a life-long process of continuous learning and improvement, you can expect to attain exponential fulfillment and accomplishments. Even when it feels as if you are taking two steps forward, one step back, as the years progress, so do you.

Now think of the areas of your life where you are stuck. Where do not achieve results you desire? Where do giant stop signs inhibit your progress? Are you baffled by your inability to get what you want?

Apply the Natural Brilliance model to your stuck areas to break through the limitations of your dysfunctional learning process. Reclaim your genius to accomplish what you desire.

This chapter will help you pull out the stop signs and reinstall Natural Brilliance where you need it most. You can learn and develop the skills essential for success.

Learn How To Learn

The purpose of using the Natural Brilliance model is to dampen the yo-yo effect of oscillation; pull out stop signs that were installed emotionally, intellectually, and physically; realize your capabilities for genius; and create a path to success.

Natural Brilliance produces outcome-based, generative learning, not therapy. Every time you progress, you also learn how to learn and how to succeed. The long-range benefit is that instead of staying stuck in oscillation, you will step into a continuous cycle of lifelong learning—Natural Brilliance.

To illustrate how you can use the Natural Brilliance model, I will give real-life examples of two people who used the Natural Brilliance to resolve their issues. I chose their stories because they deal with opposite ends of a single dilemma. Compare what results they get before and after:

Patty experiences problems balancing her career success and her intimate-relationship difficulties. A dedicated, persistent, hard-working individual, Patty receives consistent acknowledgment for her accomplishments. She has always gotten any job she has sought. When she decided to change careers, she did it easily. Patty loves her career.

Her marriage was a different story. After seven difficult years, she divorced her high school sweetheart. She has good friends, but no mate. At times, coming home to a lonely apartment makes her feel like a failure in the personal area of her life. "I'm attractive. I'm a nice person." Baffled by the incongruity between her career success and her marriage failure, she asks, "So what's wrong with me?" Patty feels everything in her life is fabulous, except when it comes to having a long-term intimate relationship with someone she loves.

Beth, on the other hand, has concentrated on being a patient, conscientious mother and wife. She and Pete have been married for 18 years. Although they have been through many difficult times, they maintain their strong commitment to each other.

Trained at the university as an art educator, Beth has never finished her degree nor pursued her career. Instead, she has sacrificed to help her husband develop his career. Ever present in her three children's lives, Beth has been PTA president, church board member, community volunteer, and school mom. Without her hard work, many of the volunteer programs that support her children's school and community would have failed.

With the youngest child now in school full-time, Beth feels empty. She knows she needs to supplement the family income to prepare for upcoming college expenses. While her husband is at the height of his professional career, Beth realizes she has done nothing in her own. She wants to work but doesn't know what skills can she offer to earn a decent wage. If she takes a full-time position, she will not be available when the kids are on spring break or summer vacation.

Trapped in the dilemma between work and family, Beth feels lost. She is a great asset to her part-time employer, but her wage hardly justifies the hassles. She loves her family, yet she feels she has wasted her career potential.

Patty and Beth are oscillating between opposing ideas: Career vs. Relationship. Both have developed significant skills in their own areas of success. When they try to make progress in their areas of weakness, however, they feel more discouraged every time they attempt a solution. The road seems endless with little hope. As Beth describes it, "The light at the end of my tunnel is just another oncoming train."

I will use Patty and Beth to illustrate how the steps of Natural Brilliance released them from their stuck states and got them on track to their goals.

Get an Attitude

In the previous four chapters, I have described how to develop the skills in each of the four steps. On the next page, in the chart of the Four Steps of Natural Brilliance, I have added three attitudes that will help incorporate the skills into your life. These attitudes and the exercises I suggest to build them come largely from my work with a model in creative and divergent thinking Dr. Frank E. Williams created more than twenty years ago.

Between releasing and noticing, **Be Receptive**; open to the magnificent opportunities that abound all around you and in you.

Between noticing and responding, **Be Generative**; create alternative interpretations and unusual options for yourself. Realize every problem has within its structure the seed of a solution. If we approach it properly, we nurture new growth in the direction of our goals.

Between responding and witnessing, **Be Persistent**; make your purpose central to your action. Experiential learning requires you to engage in living. When you show up consistently, you gain as much from your steps forward as from your steps backward.

Analyze Your Results and Step Up to Natural Brilliance

To get what you desire, you need to analyze what you have that differs from what you want, to recognize your stuck state, and to release. I am going to assume you have chosen a stuck state to play with. In some area of your life, you recognize you are not getting the results you want, and you enter a common oscillation every time you try to solve your problem.

Patty states her major life issue as a problem of establishing a long-term loving relationship. Patty tends to focus more on her career and enjoys the ease and success of her work. Meanwhile she struggles with the difficulty and discomfort of trying to establish a close personal relationship.

Her oscillation includes four components: moving toward the benefits of a loving relationship, moving toward the benefits of success on the job, moving away from the detriments of dating, and moving away from the detriments of working as the total focus of life.

With pulls toward and away from each end of the continuum between career and relationship, Patty stops.

What are you oscillating between? Go back to the description of the stuck state you created in Chapter 2 when you diagnosed your stuck state. On the worksheet that follows, fill out the blanks to add to your description.

1) What issue have you wanted to break through? Write this in the space under *The Life Issue*.

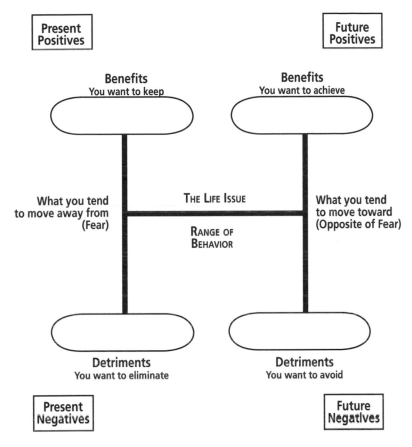

2) What opposites are fighting within you? Label what pushes you and what pulls you in your oscillation.

On the left end of the *Range of Behavior* line, write what you tend to move away from (the fear).

On the right end of the *Range of Behavior* line, specify what you tend to move toward (the opposite of the fear, which is probably your goal.)

These labels define the endpoints of what I refer to in Chapter 3 as your comfort zone, or *range of behavior.*

3) What are the benefits at each endpoint? In the stop signs above the line, write specific benefits associated with each end of the continuum.

Above the fear, write in the present positives you now enjoy These are benefits you want to keep when you change your life issue.

Above the opposite of the fear, write in the future positives you hope to enjoy. These are benefits you want to achieve by making a change in your life issue.

Benefits should be stated in positive terms. For example, "I would no longer be lonely" is not a benefit statement. "I would feel safe and loved" is stated in positive terms.

4) What are the detriments at each endpoint? In the stop signs below the line, write specific detriments associated with each end of the continuum.

Below the fear, write in the present negatives you now suffer. These are detriments you want to eliminate when you change your life issue.

Below the opposite of the fear, write in the future negatives you do not want and are afraid might show up. These are detriments you want to avoid when making a change in your life issue.

Now take a time-out. Cease struggling and allow the stress to evaporate. Remember, you cannot resolve this paradoxical problem using your typical problem-solving strategies because they put the problem into place originally.

For resources on releasing, look at the techniques in Chapter 4 and in the *Appendix*.

Be Receptive: Receive Your Genius

Stuck states cause emotional turmoil and mental confusion. Release will get you past the majority of the chronic effects of your problem situation. Happily, as you calm down, you increase your sensory awareness and your receptivity. (Also refer to Chapter 5: *Notice*.)

Now, let's really open things up.

Receive includes three discrete components: **Think Flexibly**, **Inquire**, and **Access Your Inner Mind**.

Think Flexibly

Skilled problem-solvers think flexibly to produce a variety of ideas, responses, questions, and solutions to the problems. Seek as many different directions or alternatives as you have time to consider.

When you are considering what to do about a situation, shift approaches or change direction in thinking, as you would in a car when you encounter a detour. Flexible thinkers come up with numerous different ideas.

Play with these exercises in the next few weeks, and put a check mark by each one after you do it:

- Think of various ways to use an object other than the way it is commonly used.
- Think of alternative ways to use a benefit or a detriment of your problem.
- Make up different interpretations of specific events, situations, and problems related to your issue.
- Apply a principle or concept to your life issue that has nothing to do with your issue. For example, think of choosing a career the way you would make a large purchase. What if you knew your career would be obsolete within five to ten years?
- Take another's point of view or consider situations differently from the way you normally would.
- Discuss your situation with others and take a different position from theirs.
- Think of a number of different possibilities for solving your problem.

Inquire

Skilled problem-solvers maintain curiosity, the salient characteristic of all learners. Someone who is stuck is certain. Someone solving problems inquires.

A curious person observes keenly and inquires. Find out about the people, the objects, and the situations associated with your life issue. Wonder. Give yourself time to "not know," to explore, to ask questions, and to puzzle over things for awhile.

Play with these exercises in the next few weeks, and put a check mark by each one after you do it:

- Inquire into everything, and question everyone.
- Observe your body and mind when an issue causes you to oscillate or stops you.

- Question the usually accepted way of approaching this problem area of your life.
- Search books, maps, pictures, people, and strategies, constantly looking for new ideas.
- Explore the unfamiliar.
- Use all your senses to make sense out of things.
- Probe for the subtleties of how the problem operates.
- Study the meaningful details.

Access Your Inner Mind

Skillful problem-solvers rely on their inner mind to produce answers, because they know that most of the resources for personal change and development reside there, not in the conscious mind. It is your conscious mind's attempt to solve your current problem that keeps you stuck in it. To do something new means to change brain states from conscious struggle to inner guidance. One of the themes of Natural Brilliance is the extraordinary power of the inner mind.

Making changes in brain states is a specialty of Dr. F. Noah Gordon. In his book, *Magical Classroom*, he describes three possible brain states. Like changing channels on a television, we can change our brain channels and access much more of the brain's potential for action, learning, and creativity.

You use the Action Channel when you perform physically. You misuse it if you turn to it for learning, remembering, and creating. Ironically, although the Action Channel serves you badly for answering tests in school, it is the channel most schools access. To reach the infinitely larger potential of your inner mind, the Action Channel is the worst. Use the Action Channel *after* you have resolved your stuck state with Natural Brilliance.

On the other hand, you access the Learning Channel by first passing through a "relaxation gate." Quieting your mind puts your brain into the alpha state, the home of the real learner. This calm state is a relaxed mode where you perceive directly from your sensory systems. In it you can enjoy effortless learning.

The High Creativity Channel is the "home of super abilities." In this reverie state, achieved through the practice of accessing the inner mind, you receive creative flashes, intuitive responses, and spiritual inspiration. Your genius resides here, according to Dr. Gordon. Clearly, you need to tune into this channel to create the results you want from a paradoxical problem.

While you are in touch with your inner resources, you have the opportunity to tap the cumulative genius of other great minds as well. Imagine, entering a relaxed inner state and downloading into your inner database the expert knowledge of the most brilliant thinkers on any subject you choose. From this enormous database, you can spontaneously manifest your success.

In Part 3 of this book, you will learn PhotoReading and Direct Learning, cutting-edge methods to capitalize on the vast potential of your inner mind. Ideas about how to create the results you desire will begin to bubble up. The effects may be subtle or conspicuous. PhotoReaders often recognize changes in their internal representations—their inner pictures, voice, and feelings—and their actions after PhotoReading inspirational books.

Be Generative: Create New Choices

The second step to Natural Brilliance is Notice. This is your time to gather information from the world around you and within you. If you have played with the attitudes discussed above, you are already well on your way to creating choices you never before dreamed possible.

Remember Beth in our example. She was striving to fulfill her dreams of a career. By noticing, she began to observe her beliefs regarding how much the community, the church, her children, and her husband needed her on a moment-to-moment basis. Her assumption had been that, without her, nobody else would do anything; at the same time she resented everyone for usurping her life energy.

As she noticed, she began to walk away from committees at school and fellowship circles at church and discover her priorities mattered. She maintained her power by saying that it was now up to someone else to contribute. Beth asked her husband and children to share chores.

Soon, she had time to reflect on her career. As she did so, her stop signs confronted her, wounds she had incurred in jobs after high school and during college. She realized she was afraid to put herself back into the workplace. "What if I can't do the job? What if I don't have the knowledge and skills? What if I need more education?"

Keep in mind that the goal here is not to solve the problem. The goal is to notice new options and decide how to respond differently, in a way that builds small concrete indicators of movement in the right direction. In this process of discovery resist the urge of rushing to change your life too soon. Otherwise, you will run into the same old problems. The guaranteed way to ensure your success: be generative.

Remember that with therapeutic or remedial change, you seek to fix what is broken. With the alternative of generative change, you take care of your present situation by creating your own present and future results.

Between the steps of Notice and Respond, enhancing your generative approach to problem-solving will reap enormous benefits. The components to this approach include being **motivated by complexity** and engaging in **fluent**, **original**, and **elaborative thinking**.

Seek Complexity

The first component of a generative attitude is to desire "taking on a challenge." Think of the people you know who thrive on tackling complicated situations and difficult problems. They delight in generating clever solutions.

Exercise your generative muscles over the next few weeks by applying the following challenges not only to your personal issue but also daily to your home and career. Put a check mark by each one after you do it:

- Find things to appreciate about complex ideas or problems.
- Discover intriguing aspects of messy situations.
- Delve into the most complex task first to find out what makes it complex.
- Consider the ramifications of choosing the most difficult way out.
- Figure things out for yourself, without help, in at least part of your problem.
- Enjoy the challenge of doing something that is harder for you to do than most tasks.
- Discover the thrill of doing something again and again in order to gain success.
- Be tenacious and take satisfaction in not giving up easily.
- Choose the harder problem because of its complexity.
- Seek more difficult answers rather than accepting an easy one.

Think Fluently

With the second component of being generative, a person who tends to be fluent in his or her thinking usually comes up with the most ideas, responses, solutions, or questions. They produce a quantity of ways or suggestions for doing things. It is characteristic of a fluent thinker to always think of more than one answer, and counting these alternatives determines how fluent a person is.

Here are some ways for you to exercise the cognitive skill of fluent thinking. Play with them in the next few weeks, and put a check mark by each one after you do it:

- Generate a flow of answers when you ask a question.
- Ask many questions.
- Draw several pictures when asked to draw one.
- Create numerous ideas about something while others struggle for one idea.
- Use a large number of words when expressing yourself.
- Produce more than others around you.
- Work fast, and do more than just the assignment in front of you.
- Add, subtract, multiply, and divide.
- Assume the opposite: that the false is true; the ridiculous, serious; the hilarious, sad.

Originate

Generate original ideas. Invent. Celebrate your uniqueness. Think your own thoughts. The third component of generativity celebrates your uniqueness. People who have strength in original thinking usually dream up novel solutions. They produce clever ideas rather than common or obvious ones. They delight in thinking and designing with differences, and they choose to figure things out and express them in new ways. If you could count the number of uncommon responses or productions away from the usual, you could get a measure on how original a person is.

Original thinkers tend to think of a new approach rarely thought of by others. They use their capacities to combine pieces of the usual into a new and unusual whole.

To build your strengths in original thinking, play with the following exercises. Explore them in the next few weeks, and put a check mark by each one after you do it:

- Place objects in the room off center, or explore asymmetry in drawings and designs.
- Seek a fresh approach to a stereotyped answer.
- Be different, and have a new twist in thinking or behaving.
- Enjoy the unusual, and rebel against doing things the way everyone else does them.
- Deviate from others to do things your own way.
- Figure out your own new solution.
- Invent a new way to practice a tradition.
- If the combination appeals to you, eat pickles and peanut butter together.
- Play a major key with your left hand and a minor key with your right, simultaneously.
- Delete this list, and create one of your own.

Elaborate

Generative thinkers elaborate. They want to add to or elaborate on ideas or productions. They live to stretch or expand on things. They seek to embellish materials or solutions by making them elegant and interesting. People who are elaborate in their thinking may not be originators, but once they get hold of a new idea, they modify or expand it. If you could count the number of times a person senses something lacking and adds details to improve it, you could determine how elaborative a person is.

Here are suggestions for exercising your powers of elaborative thinking. Play with these exercises in the next few weeks, and put a check mark by each one after you do it:

- Add lines, colors, and details to your own or another person's drawing.
- Sense a deeper meaning to an answer or solution by enumerating detailed components.
- Modify someone else's great idea.
- Accept an idea or someone else's work, and "jazz it up."
- Decorate something barren or plain into something beautifully fancy.
- Add dozens of ideas to this list.

The quality of responses that flow from a relaxed, aware state of mind may amaze you. Maintaining a receptive and generative approach in the way you think and behave when facing a problem will ensure you make definite strides in the direction of your goal.

Beth decided to take a job. Although it was not her first choice for furthering her career, she worked part-time doing customer service, data entry, and shipping for her husband's business. Beth rediscovered what she knew was true. She was a fast study. The part-time position allowed for flexibility with her children's school schedule, including summer vacation. Within one year, she had built such confidence and personal power, she ventured out into the career of her choice—working in homes and businesses as a professional artist. She called the woman at the top in her field. Now, while Beth apprentices, she earns money as the master's assistant.

Be Persistent: Stick to It and Keep On Keeping On

In the transition between the steps of Respond and Witness, you need to maintain an attitude of persistence. Without follow-through in your behaviors, your actions fall short of your desires. Without persistent witness, or vigilance, you may miss the real learning opportunities taking place.

For three years Patty tried to keep her relationships comfortable and successful. She chose to develop close personal relationships with men many years older who were married and unhappy in their marriages. The men loved the attention they received from this young single woman, so they created time for her. In her oscillation, these men seemed safe because they were unable to make serious commitments to her.

Noticing her pattern of going in and out of relationships, Patty began choosing to interact in new ways, outside of her comfort zone. She adopted a receptive and generative approach to the way she faced her problems and began acknowledging the price she was paying for working too hard on her career. She restructured her job contract to create more free time and travel time. She convinced the administration to hire an assistant to do the work she normally did until 10 o'clock at night.

With more free time to focus on creating a meaningful relationship, Patty started dating in new ways. She mingled outside the workplace with single, available men. She spoke her truth and stated what she wanted clearly. When a man did not respond appropriately, she learned how those situations happened. She began differentiating between fear in the other person and fault in herself, rather than shouldering all the responsibility for communicating. She allowed herself to feel the natural insecurities of relating to her companions. With every phone conversation and date, she grew in strength and personal courage.

Patty took a nurturing view of all her successes and failures. She felt as if she were stumbling along, learning to walk for the first time. Making mistakes was no longer a reason to relive the humiliation of junior high school, or a time for self-castigation and self-doubt. She realized more personal power to influence her life in the positive direction of her goal as she stepped up to her fears and accepted not doing well.

"It's amazing to me," she exclaimed, "how little permission to fail I gave myself at first. If I had avoided meaningful relationships for twenty years and had only dismal experiences to refer to before that, why should I expect immediate success?"

"When I started to relax and play, the real learning I needed began pouring into my life. Not all of it was great at the time, but I can see how every step in my development has contributed to my happiness today."

Patty fully used the steps of Respond and Witness to discover the essential attitude for both is persistence. Persistence can be thought of as having two elements—**Courage** and **Imagination**. With these two qualities, you can persistently move in the direction of your goals and witness your unfolding excellence in your successes and failures.

Take Risks with Care and Courage

Being courageous means doing something in spite of your fears. Of course, we need to take risks cautiously, after witnessing their best and worst possible results. This is where imagination comes in handy; it is a terrific way to take chances without being foolhardy.

You will find courage inherent in persistence. Courageous risk-takers willingly make guesses. They play on a hunch just to see where it will take them. Courageous people ignore failure and criticism to tackle uncertain, unconventional, and unstructured situations and problems.

To develop your powers of courage and take new strides in life, play with the following suggestions in the next few weeks. Put a check mark by each one after you do it:

- Be willing to defend your ideas regardless of what others think, even if you know you may be wrong.
- Set high goals of accomplishment without fear of going for them.
- Admit to a mistake.
- Tell the truth until you feel good.
- Tackle the difficult tasks in front of you.
- Reach for something new and difficult.
- Let go of what others might think or disapprove of about you.
- Hold fast to your choices to succeed.
- Take a chance, or dare to find out more about yourself.

Imagine

The imaginative person can conceptualize the future as something other than the past moved forward. With the power of your imagination, you can visualize and dream about things that have never happened to you. Putting your imagination first really is the only way to proceed with the faith or hope of achieving success. Without imagination, you doom yourself to repeat mistakes. Perhaps you have heard the phrase "Where there is no vision, the people will perish." Written centuries ago, it speaks ever clearer as time goes by. *Imaginative vision is the skill at the core of Natural Brilliance.*

People with a strong imagination recognize the difference between fantasy and reality and use it to their advantage. Masters of alchemy, they transform their fantastic vision into fantastic reality.

Some ways to exercise the power of your imagination follow. Play with these in the next few weeks, and put a check mark by each one after you do it:

- Tell a story about a place you can never visit.
- Intuitively feel something that has not yet happened.
- Predict what someone else has said or done without having known that person.
- Go somewhere in your dreams without leaving the room.
- Build images of things you have never seen.
- See weird shapes in a picture or drawing that the artist probably never intended.

- Wonder about something that has never happened.
- Make inanimate objects come alive.
- Read your tea leaves, and envision your fondest dreams come true.

Final Notes

As you have seen, the Natural Brilliance model leads to continuous personal improvement. It guarantees you lifelong experiential learning. The approaches suggested in this chapter have built-in safety checks; Natural Brilliance goes by the maxim "Challenge by choice." Every movement you make in life creates feedback. If you push beyond your capacity to learn, your feedback will pain you and erect more stop signs. If you stay within your capacity to relax, your feedback will intrigue you and stir your curiosity and courage.

Healthy tension, also termed *eustress* (as opposed to distress), winds its way between boredom and anxiety toward optimal learning. In that strategic zone, where your Natural Brilliance flows in a state of relaxed awareness, you can respond to your world, witness your effects, and live your life to the fullest.

Maintain your higher purpose for all that you do. When you awaken tomorrow morning, ask yourself: "What do I really want today?" At the end of your day, ask: "In what ways did I live my life on purpose?"

Stay on purpose for your highest good. In the chapters that follow, I share four of the most powerful personal and professional development strategies I know: PhotoReading, Direct Learning, Creative Problem-Solving, and the New Option Generator. Each of them relies on your Natural Brilliance. Each technique takes you to a higher-level application of the four-step Natural Brilliance model. Use each of the steps to activate everything you have learned so far. Begin choosing how you will bring your genius to fruition in your life.

To close this chapter and Part 2 of the book, I offer you a bedtime story for your conscious mind, as well as a parable for your inner mind. It's called "The Stretch Stitch."

> Once upon a time there was a wise old seamstress whose business had flourished for decades. She owned a large shop, staffed by men and women young and young at heart. The employees enjoyed a committed partnership of talents, knowledge, and creative ideas.

One day another business owner approached the seamstress and asked to what she attributed her success. She replied, "Our success is found in the lesson of the stretch stitch."

"Most of our work of joining two pieces of fabric together involves sewing a straight stitch to form a seam," the seamstress explained. "Most of the time it holds just fine, but it can break because it is brittle, rigid, and linear. If it breaks, it unravels. And that would be a problem right here," she said grabbing the man's sleeve and pointing to the seam between the sleeve and the shoulder, "Your sleeve would fall right to the floor, wouldn't it?"

"At a place like this, this place called 'on the bias,' we need something different." Pointing her finger into the visitor's chest, she added, "And you have a bias for succeeding in business, don't you?" winking at the man.

The seamstress lowered her voice into a hoarse whisper to make sure the man listened carefully and said, "The most remarkable stitch is a simple one that takes two stitches forward and one stitch back. It is both strong and flexible—more so than any other. This stitch teaches all who are ready to succeed."

She leaned forward with a meaningful gaze twinkling in her eye and continued, "Are you willing to take a step back with every few steps you take forward? Notice your progress. Learn from where you have come, and look to where you are going. You will soon develop remarkable personal strength and flexibility. With these valuable resources you will succeed in any life endeavor."

9

Activate the Natural Brilliance Model

Since starting this book, how have you challenged yourself to stretch beyond your comfort zone? You *can* rid yourself of stop signs that hold certain areas of your life in oscillation. You no longer need to be confined by past fears, limitations, or stuck states. Perhaps while you have been playing with these ideas, you have already pulled out a few stop signs and enjoyed some immediate benefits. If so, congratulations. If not, perhaps you have been waiting to get the whole picture before going ahead. I invite you to experience the many possibilities open to you now.

Part 3 brings all the principles, steps, and attitudes of Natural Brilliance together into a whole. I have suggested practical applications all along, but now I am going to present formulas—cookbook-style recipes—that anyone can use to produce tangible results. Use these simple exercises to change your unproductive patterns of behavior forever.

You will learn three new applications of Natural Brilliance: Direct Learning, Resolving Paradoxical Problems, and the New Option Generator. They offer step-by-step approaches to handling lifelong stuck states. As you experience these techniques of problem-solving and personal development, you may find immediate, sometimes inexplicable, benefits emerging in your life.

Starting with this chapter, Part 3 will prepare you to integrate Natural Brilliance as an ongoing, spontaneous response to oscillation. You will engage your body-mind to quickly achieve your goals. Instead of slogging around in problems when they arise, you can meet them on the high road. Rather than oscillating in stuck states, you can automatically trigger your desired states of thinking, feeling, and behaving, effectively engaging your Natural Brilliance.

Chapter 10 showcases the Direct Learning process. Based on the PhotoReading whole mind system, Direct Learning goes beyond PhotoReading to activate new knowledge and skills directly into your behavior. Chapter 11 teaches you how to resolve Paradoxical Problems. It introduces the Creative Problem-Solving process so that you direct your energies toward solving the correct problem.

Chapter 12 presents the culmination of the Natural Brilliance book. It guides you through seven exercises that combine Release, Notice, Respond, Witness, and every other concept of this book. The New Option Generator already has produced power-packed results for thousands of people. Watch out! This process has the potential to transform your stuck state and your life. In Chapters 13 and 14 we conclude the book with how to stay on track to your goals.

The best way to experience Part 3 is to identify a specific problem that has plagued you. Then as you learn, you can also achieve a breakthrough. Is there a stuck state too big? I think not. The Natural Brilliance model shows you how to educate yourself using your "best teacher"—experience.

If we seek the miracles of the universe, we have to welcome them when they manifest. Let me illustrate with stories of two women I know.

Open to Greater Possibilities

Despite the medical impossibility, Andrea Fisher recovered from a spinal injury that had left her quadriplegic. Her spine and spinal column had been crushed in an automobile accident. She had spent three months in a coma and three years in a hospital paralyzed. Then one day she stood up next to her bed. Now she walks well and leads a normal life.

Neurological specialists from all over the world have studied her case. She has been invited to address international congresses on neurology. The conclusion of the medical profession: her recovery was miraculous. Nothing in their science could fully explain the transformation in Andrea's neural anatomy.

The neurologist originally assigned to her case at the hospital has since left the practice of neurology to study alternative healing methods. Because his medical model could not account for what he had witnessed, he decided to search for a system of healing that could.

Andrea said to me, "You know, Paul, my recovery was not a miracle at all. It was no more a miracle than our hearts beating or our talking to each other. I can tell you exactly what I did to recover. I can describe every detail. I re-educated myself mentally, emotionally, and physically. I can tell you every therapeutic procedure I performed. But, not many people are ready to hear about it or do what it takes to get well."

Both Andrea and her neurologist openly explored how to use the enormous possibilities available to us all. The life experience of another remarkable woman, Jane Danielson, presents a slightly different message.

I met Jane for the first time when she attended an in-service training I was delivering to crisis hotline counselors. Pale and stiff then, she was wearing a T-shaped metal brace across her back and neck. Chronic pain had handicapped her like a vice since an auto accident 14 years earlier. She had tried every imaginable physical and surgical remedy. Six spinal fusion operations had left her back and neck rigid as a concrete post, throbbing mercilessly. Jane could only look straight ahead; if she wanted to look behind her, she had to turn her whole body.

Then she attended a workshop given by Moshe Feldenkrais, famous for his biomechanical approach to physical therapy. Jane managed to arrange a private session with Moshe following the conference. At the beginning of the brief session, Dr. Feldenkrais asked Jane to remove her brace. He walked his fingers up and down her spine once. Jane was still expecting a significant intervention when he told her, "Turn your head from side to side." She did!—An impossibility, given her spinal fusion operations. Pointing to the neck brace, all he said to her was, "And throw that damn thing away!" That was in 1980. To this day Jane easily swivels her head.

Jane went to her doctor's office to show him what she could do. As she entered, Jane proudly announced, "Look what I can do!" and turned her head from side to side. But her neurologist scolded her sharply. "You can't do that!"

"What do you mean?" Jane said. "Look!" and she turned her head again.

"I did the surgery on you," he said, gruffly poking his index finger into her sternum. "You can't do that!" He then turned briskly and slammed the door behind him. Jane never returned to his clinic.

Jane's story emphasizes an important point about integrating the Natural Brilliance model: we must stay open to possibilities. Andrea and Jane both instinctively understood and behaved consistent with the Natural Brilliance model of learning. The diametrical reactions from

Andrea's neurologist and Jane's neurologist show only one doctor willing to witness genius.

With the Natural Brilliance model, we learn from our experience. If we want to learn the miracles of the universe, we have to ready ourselves to receive them.

I invite you to consider, in the next few sections of this chapter, how the seemingly miraculous changes I have been promoting can occur in your life. You have the following capacities with which to knock down your stop signs and transform your possibilities into the results you desire.

- Your nonconscious mind and the preconscious processor
- Nonconscious acquisition of information
- Newly discovered pathways to the inner mind
- Implicit memory

Now that you have read the list of the wonders you already possess, I want to lay out the new procedures I have designed for you to activate the full power of your Natural Brilliance.

Use the Nonconscious Mind and Preconscious Processor

Do you know who you really are? You are a living, feeling, thinking, learning being. By every measure, you are magnificent! You have at your disposal two remarkable tools, at once unbelievably complex and patently simple—your *nonconscious mind* and your *preconscious processor*. The Natural Brilliance model suggests an ideal approach to using them to your immediate benefit.

The nonconscious part of our brain processes information and stores memory. According to educational psychologist Dr. Win Wenger, its database outweighs that of the conscious mind by ten billion to one. The pathway into this phenomenal capacity of mind is called the *preconscious processor*. Many times faster than the conscious mind, the preconscious processor continually scans billions of bits of data, determining what is important and what is not. When it notes something important, it immediately signals the conscious mind to pay attention.

As you already have a nonconscious mind and a preconscious processor and you still have problems, the question remains, how can you use them to benefit your daily life? Using the PhotoReading whole mind system for

Direct Learning will provide you with a powerful answer to that question. In 1986, I developed the PhotoReading course to effectively use these two capacities of mind and solved a huge problem for people trapped by information overload.

With PhotoReading you can mentally photograph the written page faster than a page a second. Now, PhotoReaders worldwide comprehend and retain information in a fraction of the time they used to spend regular reading. The power of the human mind demonstrated with PhotoReading has inspired many graduates of the program to ask, "If I can PhotoRead, what else can I do?"

Over the years of watching people learn about their great capacities, I realized that the personal development opportunities for PhotoReaders go far beyond processing written information efficiently. PhotoReading and Direct Learning awaken us to the vast abilities of mind. At first we blink into the light. Then we begin to see we do not have to wait for authority or approval. On our own, we can release, notice, respond, and witness the Natural Brilliance we already possess.

Acquire Information and Skills Nonconsciously

According to research done at the cognitive laboratory at Tulsa University, the human brain can acquire information and skills nonconsciously.

The work done by Dr. Pawel Lewicki suggests that the human cognitive system nonconsciously detects and processes information. His studies provide evidence that subjects in experiments have no access to the newly acquired procedural knowledge and no idea that they have learned anything from the stimulus material, even though the newly acquired knowledge consistently guides their behavior.

Dr. Lewicki has also determined that with preconscious processing, the inner mind is "incomparably more able to process complex knowledge faster and 'smarter' overall than our ability to think and identify meanings of stimuli consciously."

In a journal article, he wrote, "Most of the 'real work,' both in the acquisition of cognitive procedures and skills and in the execution of cognitive operations, is being done at the level to which our consciousness has no access. The sophistication and speed of this inner processing far exceed what can even be approached by our consciously controlled thinking."

Even more provocative is his conclusion. "The 'responsibility' of this inaccessible level of our mental functioning is more than routine operations such as retrieving information from memory and adjusting the level of arousal. It is directly involved in the development of interpretive categories, drawing inferences, determining emotional reactions, and other high-level cognitive operations."

Dr. Lewicki's work indicates to me that using nonconscious acquisition of information promises our best opportunities to change and grow. In Chapter 10, I present a breakthrough technique for self-development combining PhotoReading with Direct Learning to activate your inner wisdom.

PhotoReading massive amounts of information helps the inner mind notice new options. Activation with Direct Learning provides a way to respond without *trying* to respond differently. Because Direct Learning changes behavior without your conscious intervention to change your behavior, it breaks the cycle of your paradoxical problems. The change occurs indirectly from inner wisdom working beyond conscious logic to solve your problems. It's paradoxically perfect and ideally suited to your life.

Discover New Pathways into the Body-Mind

Supportive evidence for the breakthroughs of PhotoReading and Direct Learning came from PhotoReader Dr. Izzy Katzeff, a senior lecturer of neurophysiology at the University of Witwatersrand Medical School in Johannesburg, South Africa. While he was recovering from a stroke, he made a remarkable personal discovery. His stroke had created a lesion in his primary visual cortex (V1), resulting in *posterior alexia*. He could still write, but he could not read. Although he could not comprehend written material, he could readily recognize words spelled aloud or words spelled on the palm of his hand.

After two and a half frustrating months when he could not even recognize any printed letters of the alphabet, he turned to PhotoReading. Instantly he began to read and comprehend what he had PhotoRead. Ecstatic, he called me to report that after PhotoReading five books, he could once again read in a regular manner.

"The only way this is possible," he said, "is if we possess some *neural pathway that bypasses the primary visual cortex.* This proves it, and it demonstrates that PhotoReading is the way to access this pathway. This is exactly what you have said all along by referring to the *preconscious processor* and the *nonconscious* mind. This cements it, because I have a physical lesion and there is no way I can consciously perceive the page without a bypass. PhotoReading makes it possible."

About six months later I got another excited call from Izzy. "I just read an article in a journal of neurology that proves my hypothesis, Paul. The article shows clinical research that demonstrates conscious perception of information is possible without the primary visual cortex. They have located the very pathway we were talking about."

I went to the biomedical library at the University of Minnesota. Sure enough, the article "Conscious Visual Perception without V1" by university researchers Barbur, Watson, Frackowiak, and Zeki in London reveals groundbreaking research of brain lesion studies. The authors submit, in the journal *Brain*, that neural pathways exist that scientists had not previously recognized. Izzy was right! We had already been teaching the PhotoReading whole mind system based on that hypothesis eight years before the research was available with a neurological explanation.

In other words, more pathways connect your brain to behavior than most of your teachers ever imagined or encouraged you to access. However, in order to account for Direct Learning, we still need an explanation for *how* we route information to the brain to get new behaviors out, all without conscious involvement. Here again, Dr. Izzy Katzeff pointed the way.

In the early 1950s, Dr. Brenda Milner collaborated with Dr. Wilder Penfield on studying Penfield's brain lesion patients from the 1940s. Milner discovered that human memory involves multiple memory systems. She wanted to account for how a stroke patient could learn a task one day and by the next day forget having ever done the task. Somehow the patient would still retain the learning, building skills with the task over successive days. Her studies led to the distinction between implicit and explicit memory.

Your body-mind comes fully equipped for implicit memory, which bypasses the conscious mind altogether. You already have the "wetware" programmed to express the benefits of implicit learning, as evidenced by PhotoReading and Direct Learning.

Does it bother you that you were born with all these remarkable abilities, yet no one ever told you how to use them? Dr. Norman F. Dixon, retired professor from the University College in London, heralded our human potential in the early 1970s. His book, entitled *Subliminal Perceptions: The Nature of a Controversy,* shook the academic and psychological community.

In Dixon's words, "If the hypothesis that people can be affected by stimuli of which they cannot be aware is valid, then it has profound implications not only for the psychophysiology of memory, perception, emotion, motivation, and dreams but also for the nature of consciousness itself."

The evidence has been mounting that humans have unlimited mental capacity. Still, Dr. Dixon told me in our conversations about implicit learning, the academic community remains firmly unconvinced. For certain, successful personal experiences in implicit learning will prove to your conscious mind that your brain already possesses the capacities I have been describing. I designed the Natural Brilliance model for you so you can be your own best teacher. Now more than ever, like spinal injury patients Andrea and Jane, you can take independent steps to fill your life with all the learning you desire.

Do It!

In the next chapter I present how to use PhotoReading and Direct Learning to acquire the knowledge and skills you need for powerful life change. Plan to do the techniques as outlined, because, most likely, your own results will be your greatest convincers. Do it and witness the results you produce.

Leap over Performance Barriers with Direct Learning

"Take two giant steps and leap."
"Captain, may I?"
Remember that game from your childhood? If we played the game now, I would assure you "Yes, you may!"

The two giant steps I refer to are two learning processes I developed: PhotoReading, to input information faster than a page a second; and Direct Learning, to transmute intrinsic learning into new behaviors and improved skills aligned with your life purpose. The leap I refer to is the quantum leap toward your goals you can enjoy right away.

Direct Learning involves PhotoReading several books on a single topic and having the benefits of the information translate directly into new behaviors and improved skills. Direct Learning bypasses the need for consciously activating the knowledge from the texts through cognitive channels. I shall take you through the five steps of the PhotoReading whole mind system as a prerequisite of Direct Learning.

If you are not currently a PhotoReader, read the next section of this chapter to understand how it works. Then, at least spend an evening with my book *PhotoReading* to develop your skills as a PhotoReader.

Learn How to PhotoRead

PhotoReading is a breakthrough technology for processing written information. People around the world are using it to access their Natural Brilliance. With the PhotoReading whole mind system, you can learn what you need from any written materials in a fraction of the time it would normally take you.

You can transform your reading from procedures into creative new options. Release your genius in five easy steps: Prepare, Preview, PhotoRead, Postview, and Activate. After I guide you briefly through these steps in this chapter, you can apply PhotoReading to this book and other written materials right away—today.

PhotoReading applies the Natural Brilliance model totally. As an approach to written materials, it naturally releases the built-in stops installed when you first learned to read. Elementary school taught us to read perfectly, to sound out every word, and "Oops, oops, go back, you missed something!" to not miss a thing. If we missed a word in school, most of us were programmed to stop, go back, and make sure we comprehended and remembered every word as we went. Less than perfect was not good enough.

No wonder people maintain stacks of books and magazines, reports and journals, memos and files rather than read them. Or start reading them but never finish. Do you have any piles around your bed, dresser, desk, or credenza? Do you ever take home papers in your briefcase that you absolutely must get to tonight, only to haul them back to work unread?

With PhotoReading you break through the dysfunction of traditional reading approaches and multiply the pleasure of regular reading. As you let go of perfectionist reading attitudes, you gain access to your brilliance. The system turns on tremendous learning power, using both your conscious and nonconscious minds simultaneously. So, pull out your stop signs and move through your reading at optimum brain-speed.

A quick run through should help you get into the swing of PhotoReading now.

Prepare for Reading and PhotoReading

The first step of the PhotoReading whole mind system is also the best first step for any reading you do. *Prepare* means establish your purpose for reading and get into an ideal state for the brain to process incoming information. This step lays the foundation for efficient and effective reading.

Before reading, take a moment to think of what you want to achieve. You learn more and enjoy your reading more if you turn reading into an outcome-oriented event. Make your outcomes explicit. Do you want general or specific information? How much time are you willing to invest to achieve your goal? If you read purposefully, you are active and questioning, which will be reflected in the results you get from your reading session.

Getting into the *ideal state of mind* means entering the relaxed state of awareness that we have been playing with earlier in this book. The ideal learning channel operates on the alpha brain wave frequencies, optimum for inputting information.

Preview

Step 2 in the PhotoReading whole mind system is *Preview.* You may remember how to preview from school. Although it is the simplest of all advanced reading strategies, only requiring a few moments to perform, I know few adults who made a habit of previewing until they took the PhotoReading course. Graduate PhotoReaders appreciate the efficiency it produces in their everyday reading.

Previewing allows you to gain perspective on your reading materials and their value to you. It has three components.

First, briefly look over the written material to get an overall sense of it. Look at the front and back covers or flaps and the table of contents to ascertain its structure and context. Keep the process quick and cursory to alert your mind to what is coming and whet your curiosity.

Second, appraise the value for your purpose. Ask yourself whether the material is right for you or relevant for the purpose you initially set. Unless you learn to discern quickly which materials will serve you best, you can become bogged down in reading words that contribute little or nothing to your purpose.

Third, determine to go or not go further. This is an important decision point. If the material appears to have no value for you, it is time to stop. If the material has value for you, decide if you want to keep the same purpose or change it slightly in response to the new information you acquired during the preview.

I must tell you that although previewing helps, it can trap you if stay too long and aim to get too much information. Some readers use previewing to try to understand a written piece completely. Expecting to get everything consciously too soon will shut off access to the nonconscious mind, which we must use if we are going to break through the limitations of the conscious mind.

To prevent such a shutdown of the vast resources of your inner mind, I suggest that you hardly preview at all. Take only one to two minutes before PhotoReading to know that you want to read the text. Then, immediately after PhotoReading (which you will learn next), you will more thoroughly review the materials. This approach keeps your inner mind engaged and facilitates preconscious acquisition of information and effective learning and comprehension.

Take a minute or two to preview this book, if you have not already done so. Previewing it now will give you an opportunity to notice a difference in your reading efficiency in the rest of this book.

Follow the PhotoReading Procedure

Here are the six components of PhotoReading, the third step of the PhotoReading whole mind system. Follow this procedure, and you will mentally photograph written pages at rates exceeding a page a second.

Prepare

Before beginning to PhotoRead (or regular read), always state your purpose. Clearly state to yourself what you expect to get from the materials.

Enter the Resource Level of Mind

Enter the resource level, a relaxed state of alertness for learning, using the 3-2-1 relaxation procedure.

Affirm Concentration, Impact, and Purpose

Give yourself a series of positive affirmations that will direct the material you PhotoRead to your inner mind and ensure it has the effect you desire. For example:

"As I PhotoRead, my concentration is absolute."

"All that I PhotoRead makes a lasting impression on my inner mind and is available to me."

"I desire the information in this book, (state the title of the book to yourself) to accomplish my goal of (state your purpose for reading this book).

Enter the PhotoFocus State

Bring your point of awareness to a place a few inches above and behind your head. To accomplish this, imagine the feeling of a tangerine resting on the top, back part of your head.

As you open your eyes, relax your vision and look right through the center of the book. Notice the four corners of the book as well as the space between the paragraphs. Comfortably focus your eyes beyond the book until you see the "blip" page or "cocktail weenie" page.

Maintain a Steady State While Flipping Pages

Turn your attention to your deep, even breathing. Turn the pages of the book before your eyes in a steady rhythm. Chant to the rhythm of your page-turning by mentally repeating:

"Re-lax...Re-lax. Four-Three-Two-One.

Re-lax...Re-lax. Keep the state...See the page."

Close with Mastery

Affirm your mastery of the material you have just PhotoRead:

"I acknowledge all feelings evoked by this experience and allow my inner mind and body to process them. I'm curious in how many ways I will notice this information supporting me."

Invite the conscious mind to let go while your inner mind processes all that you have PhotoRead.

There you have it. To PhotoRead: prepare, enter, affirm, PhotoFocus, maintain state, and close. I encourage you to revisit the components of "enter" and "PhotoFocus," which were partially explained earlier in this book. Entering the resource level is the state of relaxed alertness described in Chapter 4: *Release* (See section subtitled "Deep Relaxation"). I emphasize giving yourself the 3-2-1 signal to facilitate entry into this state in the future. The PhotoFocus state was described as "second sight" in Chapter 5: *Notice* (See section subtitled "Enhancing the Visual Sense").

I invite you to PhotoRead this book now if you have not already done so. PhotoReading offers many benefits. It will make the book easy to read and comprehend, and most importantly, support your activation of all the skills you desire to gain.

Make a Note About Postview and Activation

The next step of the PhotoReading whole mind system is Postview. Here you playfully explore the reading materials more thoroughly to locate areas where you want more detail. You notice key words and phrases and formulate questions for the author. Your goal is to learn enough about the materials to plan your activation, the final step of the PhotoReading whole mind system.

Activation purposefully and actively connects the conscious mind to the vast database you have created at an inner level by PhotoReading. Doing so gives you the comprehension you need in the time you have available, effectively fulfilling your purpose for reading. The major techniques of activation include Review Questions, Super Read and Dip, Skitter, Rapid Read, and Mind Map. All involve consciously interacting with the physical text you have PhotoRead.

Direct Learning does not rely on postview or conscious activation; Direct Learning represents a unique new form of activation. In the sections that follow you will learn how to use it for your personal benefit. You can achieve results from Direct Learning even if you are a beginning PhotoReader. You do need to develop the easy skill of relaxing your vision as you flip pages before your eyes and to muster a bit of trust that your nonconscious mind is performing even when you are consciously unaware of its activity.

You may not know that you are PhotoReading correctly at this point. I recommend that you "Just do it." Trust your inner mind to do the work for you, whether or not your conscious mind knows how the learning occurs. There are ways of knowing that you are PhotoReading correctly. Reading my book *PhotoReading* can help you. Certainly the *PhotoReading* personal learning course can coach you to perform the steps effectively. Ideally, take the PhotoReading seminar from an instructor certified by Learning Strategies Corporation. Nothing beats an experienced guide.

At this point, I will assume you are set to proceed with Direct Learning activation. Ready for a miracle?

Discover Direct Learning

Many PhotoReading graduates report having spontaneously improved their skill in tennis, golf, racquetball, piano playing, time management, public speaking, to name a few. Invariably, they demonstrate improvements after Syntopic Reading, a process in the *PhotoReading* book and course that teaches how to PhotoRead and activate three to five books during a single exercise.

To explore the benefits of syntopic reading and activation, Chris Sedcole, of New Zealand, created an exercise for a group of executives. He directed them to PhotoRead five books on an area of personal or professional development—three books directly related to the topic, two indirectly. For example, one participant who wanted to improve time management skills selected three books on time management, one on improving business communications, and one on delegation.

In the final step, Chris led the clients to imagine a time in the future when they had already integrated their desired new behaviors.

One month later in a follow-up session, Chris inquired if they had noticed anything in their behavior related to the exercise. Without exception, the clients reported they had experienced changes for the better. Curiously, they also said they had made no conscious attempts to improve.

PhotoReading requires that you specify your purpose. For Direct Learning select books that have ideas you have a strong personal desire to learn. Each book represents the author's reading of many books. Think of the combined years of experience you have access to when you PhotoRead five books on a single topic. If each book represents several years of the author's knowledge and skills and the essential ideas from twenty books, think what you are downloading into your neural circuitry. Direct Learning is like spending decades consulting with masters who support you in achieving the results you desire.

Unless you notice different choices available to you, you cannot respond differently. The more beneficial choices you have to select from, the more accurate a response you can make. By PhotoReading several books on a single subject, you can influence a change in the right direction, because your nonconscious mind can perceive new paths that your conscious mind, with its filters and limitations, cannot. When you input essential knowledge that distinguishes an expert from a beginner, you open yourself to activating new patterns of success.

Activate Direct Learning

For Direct Learning to be most effective, you must know what new behaviors you desire. The more specific you can be, the better this process will work. Once you have chosen your goal, select several books that speak authoritatively about the subject. It is important that these books not be theoretical. Choose practical, how-to books that teach the new behaviors you want.

I recommend you select books that approach the skills you want from multiple angles. For example, if you want to improve your close personal relationships, select three books that deal directly with intimate relationships or communications and two or three that approach the issue metaphorically. A book on creativity with a problem-solving approach might open you to communicating insightfully. You might select a book on hypnotism to gain insight into how your language is programming the results you are getting from others, or a book on building self-esteem to improve your appreciation of yourself and others. You might choose a book on financial management. Why? Maybe communicating effectively is like investing for the future. What should you know about making sound investment decisions that applies to your intimate relationships?

After selecting your books, PhotoRead them. Remember to state your purpose clearly before each book and to say a solid closing affirmation after each one. It may be a good idea to take a brief stretch or drink some water between books. Allow yourself to remain centered and relaxed throughout the process. If something happens to distract you between books, take a few moments to get back into state.

The next step is the Direct Learning activation stage. The information will be activated spontaneously in the appropriate contexts only after you direct your inner mind to generate the behaviors. Remember how you imagined doing things as a child? You called it *"Playing Pretend."* Gestalt therapists call it *"Playing As If."* See a mental simulation of the future, which encodes the brain with the necessary information to give rise to the behaviors according to your needs.

Follow the simple procedure outlined below to put in place the new behaviors you desire. If you like, make an audio recording in your voice of the component steps so you can perform them with your eyes closed.

{Begin}

Sit back in a comfortable position with your feet resting on the floor and your hands resting gently on your lap without your thumbs touching each other. Become aware of your deep even breathing, and set aside this time as your time for integrating the beneficial new behaviors and choices you desire, to achieve the results that are important to you.

Using the following procedure, enter the resource level of mind.

Take a deep breath....Hold it for a moment....As you slowly exhale, close your eyes. Think of the number 3, and mentally repeat the word *Relax*. Imagine a wave of relaxation flowing downward throughout your entire body, from the top part of your head down to the soles of your feet.

You can let this wave flow downward several times if need be. You are in charge. Any time you desire to relax as deep or deeper than now, you can do so by thinking of your physical relaxation signal, the number 3 and the word *Relax*. You are in charge of your physical relaxation.

{Pause}

Take another deep breath....Hold it a moment....Slowly exhale, think of the number 2, and mentally repeat the word *Relax*. Let go of thoughts about the past or future, focus your awareness on the present moment in time, right here, right now.

{Pause}

With each breath you breathe, let go more and relax even deeper. Imagine your consciousness expanding into this present moment.

Whenever you desire to relax as deep or deeper than now, you can do so by thinking of the number 2 and mentally repeating the word *Relax*.

{Pause}

Take another deep breath....Hold it for a moment....Slowly exhale, mentally hear the sound of the number *1*, and imagine a beautiful plant or flower.

{Pause}

This is a signal indicating that you have focused your awareness within, to this accelerated learning state. Here you have access to an expanded level of creativity and perceptual ability. You are in contact with the abundant resources of your inner mind.

Imagine yourself relaxing in a beautiful quiet scene, as if you were sitting or lying back in a peaceful place, relaxing, and enjoying this time of comfort.

{Pause}

Imagine that you can perceive yourself on your life's timeline. Your past extends in one direction, perhaps to the left or behind you. And in another direction your future extends before you, perhaps to your right. However you perceive your timeline is fine for you. Simply imagine the present moment. Where you are right now is the present. And you can comfortably glance into the past and/or into the future from where you are now.

Continue to use your creative imagination now as you float gently up over your timeline, way up over it to gain new perspective. Imagine you can see your life's path far below. Back there in your past you can imagine the events leading up to the present situation of your life. And extending another way is your future, bright and full of possibilities.

Imagine floating out into the future, over the future part of your timeline. Go all the way out over the time when you are successfully achieving the results you had specified. Below you there in your life, you are enjoying the success you desire. You can use all the new behaviors you need to accomplish the results you have chosen.

At a rate that is comfortable for you, imagine drifting gently downward onto your timeline and into your own body, experiencing the new behaviors that help you.

{Pause}

Feel how good it feels to enjoy the success of your accomplishments. See through your own eyes the success you had desired now as a reality in your life. What good things do you say to yourself with your own inner dialogue? How do you walk, what does success feel like in your head, shoulders, and body as you enjoy your success?

You can look back to the path that brought you to this point of success and accomplishment in your life. Imagine two or three of the significant events that have led to your achievement. If you like, float gently up over your timeline to get an even better perspective on the path you selected to accomplishing your goals. Notice the significant events, your successful responses, and the power and motivation you displayed to have achieved the results you had desired.

{Pause}

Take your time to make all the realizations you need and solidify all the learning that ensures your success.

{Pause}

When you feel complete with your imaginings, float back to the present moment in time and back into your quiet place. Take a few moments to enjoy all the positive and constructive ideas from your own imagination and from the books that you have PhotoRead, becoming fully integrated, automatically and spontaneously available to you in all the appropriate settings, whenever you want or need them.

Feel yourself let go for a few moments, as all the ideas and new behaviors of your choosing integrate, so that they become fully available, just as you need them to be.

{Pause}

When you are ready, bring your attention from your quiet place to an outwardly directed state of awareness by mentally counting forward from *1* to *5*. At the last number, open your eyes and return, refreshed, revitalized, and feeling good.

You can use this process after PhotoReading and after activating books consciously as well. We choose not to activate books consciously in the Direct Learning technique because the conscious mind interferes. Most people in our culture have been raised by the "Puritan Work Ethic," which means "You must work hard to achieve rewards." In athletics we say, "No pain, no gain." Direct Learning challenges traditional assumptions by demonstrating the inner mind can provide a "path of least resistance" to our success. As living life effortlessly is a real human option for the first time in history, why not do it?

Keep It Simple

Realizing how easy Direct Learning is and how much benefit it brings, you may wonder why most people never do it. Unfortunately, it is so deceptively simple that most people never even consider trying it. In fact, I had to be convinced myself. Only after the reports of PhotoReading graduates did I purposefully choose this powerful technique for my own benefit.

To review the Direct Learning process, think of the simple phrase, "*What do I want?*" When you can answer that question with clarity, you are already well on your way to accomplishing your desire. The next step is to PhotoRead a stack of books that encourage the use of the skills you need. Finally, automatically generate the new behaviors you need by visualizing your future success. Imagine yourself now in the future, in the moment of enjoying the accomplishment of your goal.

Throughout the Direct Learning process, you can see the four steps of Natural Brilliance repeating. Each cycle brings you to greater release, greater choice, greater power to respond, and higher levels of witness.

When you realize the inner mind is your ally in personal and professional development, you can begin to ask, "What else is my mind capable of doing?" The inner mind is a preverbal mind. Like a genie, it communicates through behaviors and imagery. If you ask it to help, it will demonstrate what wonders it can do for you.

When my first son, Ben, was ten months old, he could toddle, but he could not talk yet. My wife, Libby, and I attended a support group for first-time parents, where we heard a story from another couple. They said they had asked their baby daughter to follow a complex set of instructions, to which she had responded perfectly.

The next day, Libby said, "Ben, will you go over to those shoes and bring Momma her slippers?" Ben stood up and toddled over to the other end of the bedroom. He picked out the slippers from a row of six pairs and happily carried them back to her. "Amazing!" Libby and I looked at each other in shock and said, "Hey! We had never thought to ask!"

If our child were too young to speak, we reasoned that he was too young to comprehend complex ideas or carry out complex commands. How wrong we were. The following day I started him emptying the garbage and mowing the lawn. Just kidding.

The educator Eric Jensen wrote in his book *Super Teaching*, "Everyone has genius capacity. It is the context that determines the evidence." That sums it up. The inner mind needs clear requests and the impetus to act. Given the proper context, it will prove that you have abilities for genius. Do not be fooled by appearances. You have a preverbal ally, waiting to help.

Find Evidence of Success

You may ask, "How will I know I am doing this right? How will I know it's working? Immediately after the technique, I will feel good, but has anything changed?"

Paradoxically, if every day you ask yourself, "Is it working yet?" you will never notice a shift. If you pull up a seedling every day to see if it is growing, will it grow?

The changes you make with Direct Learning run deep, because you influence the unconscious control processes, which direct your habitual behavior. Because the changes integrate at a nonconscious level, at first they may be so subtle that you may think nothing has changed.

One way to witness the effects of Direct Learning is to live life normally and notice any indicators of movement in the direction of your goal. Enhance your witness perspective through feedback from others.

Those who know you well will see changes in you before you notice them in yourself.

Trust Your Inner Mind

Fear sets up the biggest stop signs of all. Some people are leery of letting go of their critical-judging mind. If they cannot make change happen by conscious volition and willpower, they consider it too risky to entrust to the inner mind. But, when you distrust your mind, you distrust yourself. Being afraid to use the full potential of your brain stops you in your tracks. Early painful experiences may have erected stop signs in the first place, but you have chosen to keep them there. Fortunately, you have the power to choose how you will live today. Choose freedom now.

Approach Paradoxical Problems with Creative Problem-Solving

Appropriate to a paradoxical situation, I begin this chapter with a riddle. I first ran into this in D.N. Perkins's book *The Mind's Best Work*. See if you can figure it out:

> There is a man at home. He is wearing a mask. There is a man coming home. What is happening in this scene?

Please notice the internal representation you create from this riddle. What did you imagine? Did you imagine a burglary scene? If not, what happened inside you when I suggested it?

Did you imagine a costume party? How about trick-or-treat on Halloween?

Each time I offer another suggestion, notice what happens to your own internal representation. The mind instantly incorporates the redefined problem (what kind of mask is being worn?) to generate a different solution (scene of what is happening). But do you have the solution yet? Notice your feelings. When everything comes together, you will experience a "felt shift," a strong internal experience of everything "fitting" together into the correct solution.

Now let's consider what obstacles are standing in the way. We can think of these as variables in the riddle that we need to change or to hold constant. So far we have changed the variable of "mask" and probably also "man." We could manipulate mask in other ways. For example, all the masks we have suggested so far have been disguises. How about a welder's mask, or a surgeon's mask? Those are masks of protection. As you consider them, notice how your scene changes.

What if the mask were abstract, as in "the mask of personality?" How might that change your scene?

One variable that we have not manipulated at all is "home." In all our scenes, the home is a house—a dwelling place. What if it were abstract, such as "Home is where the heart is"? That metaphor would change the scene.

What other kinds of "homes" are there? How about home base? Or, home plate? There is a man at home plate, wearing a mask (a catcher's mask), there is a man coming home...from third base. What is happening in this scene? It is a baseball game!

Now check your feelings. When the internal representation changed in a way that everything fit, did you feel the shift inside you? That "felt shift" is key to knowing that you have defined the correct problem.

For many years of working with clients on personal development issues, I kept posing myself a riddle: Why do people set themselves up for failure when they want to resolve a problem that affects them personally. I came to realize people set themselves up for failure when they think they are applying a new solution but are only doing more of the same. They blindly step into a trap of their own devising; self-designed and self-set, they spring it upon themselves—all the while trying to do the "right thing." They trap themselves with their unconscious problem-solving strategy, which created the problem to begin with. The faulty strategy creates the paradoxical problem.

Here are examples of two clients who came to me trapped in classic paradoxical problems. The first client, named Bob, called my office to explain his problem like this:

"Over the years I've spent thousands of dollars on self-improvement programs. I don't think that any of them has ever done me the least bit of good. In fact, I honestly believe that audio programs can't help me." He paused for a moment, perhaps underscoring a challenge to me. "Now I have your brochure, and I was wondering which of your Paraliminal sessions I should use to get past this belief?"

Do you recognize the dilemma Bob presented? There was no way I could fill his paradoxical request. As *no* self-improvement program would work for him, *any* self-improvement program I suggested would also not work. Bob had set himself up to *win* by proving himself right but, once again, *end up losing* by not being able to use the wisdom on a program to achieve his desired result.

The other client was a woman named Claire. Many years ago she came to my office wanting to lose approximately seventy pounds. Although she ate good foods, kept her diet to a minimum number of calories, exercised regularly, she stayed heavy. In discussing her experiences battling weight, Claire shared a revealing story about the nature of her stuck state.

About five years earlier Claire's husband, whom she had since divorced, had insisted that she seek medical help to lose weight. The doctor put her in a hospital for one week of extensive metabolic and hormonal testing, feeding her only intravenously. She was furious but helpless to change her imprisonment. Once committed to the hospital, all she could do was endure the testing.

Even with all the tests, the doctor could find no medical reason for Claire's condition. What's more, to the complete bafflement of the doctor and her husband, she had *gained* nine pounds during her stay. "Anyone else," the doctor told her, "would have lost at least ten to fifteen pounds."

Think about it. What better way for Claire to get even with the doctor and her husband? Get even by baffling them. Unfortunately, five years later, her strategy was still working perfectly to keep her overweight and stuck.

Run Hard to Stay in Place

Paradoxical problems, such Bob's and Claire's, elude the person who has them. A problem exists as an unintentional by-product of a solution to a different problem. Because the solution worked in one context, the body-mind offers the same behaviors to a different problem.

Naturally, when we learn something that succeeds, we prize it as an efficient, successful strategy. Our neurophysiology is designed to remember what works. But what works to solve one problem does not necessarily solve the next. In Bob's and Claire's cases, the misapplied strategy creates a unique class of stuck states—one we have only alluded to so far in this book. This oscillation is not the same as getting stopped in learning, then fearing to go on. This is an unique type of problem where being right is wrong. Clinging to the last set of skills prevents a solution to the next problem.

In a way, the oscillation inside paradoxical problems erects invisible stop signs. No specific fear—physically, emotionally, or intellectually—sends us back the way we came. We perceive, clearly enough, the detriments of our current problem situation, but we do not perceive at all that our behaviors cause those detriments. Causation seems mysteriously beyond our control.

Now, consider how perfectionism causes paradoxical dilemmas. Doing something well has its rewards. The brain, taking that learning to its illogical extreme, assumes that doing something *perfectly* will yield *optimum* rewards. If we generalize such a learning, as in the problems described earlier, we succeed at escalating error. The perfectionist insists that only flawless execution is good enough performance, anything else is failure. Either success or dismal failure—a two-point loop—resulting in oscillation.

Such oscillations occur most frequently when people get into a "do-to-be" trap—trying to feel better about themselves by working hard to perform perfectly. A client of mine named Pat had tenuous self-esteem because he continually compared his efforts to others who had achieved success. As he tried hard to feel good about himself, he tended to overcontrol his behavior, like the kid learning to drive the stick shift car in traffic on hills. What I discovered working with Pat and others like him was that the way out of paradoxical problems is also the way out of perfectionism, "do-to-be" traps, and barriers to self-esteem.

Now let's explore how to overcome the tendency to fall into paradoxical problems, how to identify them if we do, and how to understand them well enough to resolve them.

Solve Dilemmas and Resolve Paradoxical Problems

A story is told of the late great psychiatrist Dr. Milton H. Erickson when he was a young boy on his father's dairy farm in Wisconsin. As I remember the story, the weather was turning for the worse, and temperatures of minus twenty degrees Fahrenheit were threatening the livestock. Milton's father had managed to get all the cows into the barn except one. This one obstreperous cow stopped at the threshold of the barn and wouldn't budge.

Poor farmer Erickson did everything he could think of to get that cow to go into the safe warm barn, but his every attempt failed. He pushed, he pulled, he whipped, he grabbed, and he kicked without success. The harder he tried, the funnier the whole scene became to young Milton, to the point where Milton was rolling in hysterics in the snow, watching his father's increasing frustration.

Finally, Milton's father turned and shouted, "Well, if you think it's so darn funny, why don't you put the cow in the barn!"

With that, Milton leaped up and ran behind the cow. Then, grabbing its tail in both hands, he pulled as hard as possible away from the barn. Instantly, the cow mooed and leaped into the barn.

In this story the problem was not solved the way the problem was originally defined by the person in the stuck state. In reality, the problem was re-solved, or resolved, by redefining what the problem was—the paradoxical behavior at the heart of the matter—and changing it.

Write a New Story

If we go back to Claire's weight loss example, we find two issues. A self-esteem issue for her, plus an issue about how to assert her authority over her own body in a marriage that was not working for her.

In our session together, I helped her connect her experience in the hospital with her intention to get even. When she realized her weight loss had little or nothing to do with diet, she quit chastising herself for failing at weight loss. Instead, we focused on developing her sense of self as an independent, self-sufficient person, enjoying her ideal weight. In the process she let go of the excess emotional baggage she had been dragging around regarding the doctor and her ex-husband.

In follow-up conversations I had with her in months and years to come, Claire did beautifully. She had dropped over ninety pounds and successfully kept it off by habitually eating in the same low-calorie fashion she had become comfortably used to.

Bob, the self-improvement program buyer, also made a significant breakthrough. When he asked me to suggest a Paraliminal, I told him, "Bob, you need to understand that no audio program is going to change you. You've been buying programs expecting them to get you to change things about yourself, but you're right. No program has changed you or ever will change you. The only thing that can change you is you."

Evidently, Bob experienced a felt shift when he took in the truth of that statement. All along he had known he had to be in charge of his life, but he desperately wished for the magic elixir promoted in some self-improvement advertisements. "When you are ready to change yourself," I continued, "you will understand that the Paraliminal sessions can facilitate your process. They create an environment—a time and place, if you will—in which you can identify resources already in you. They do not put anything into you that is not already there. They help you gain access to it."

In recommending three Paraliminal sessions, I insisted that he use them according to my instructions or return them for a refund. I would not allow him to deceive himself into thinking the Paraliminals were going to do any work for him that he was unable or unwilling to do for himself. Bob gratefully purchased the Paraliminals and later reported he was accomplishing goals that had eluded him for years.

Both Claire and Bob like authoring their own lives. Only *they* have the authority to change their life stories. But until they recognized they were in charge, they were powerless. Did I *give* them anything? Did they *do* anything differently from what they had already been doing? Ironically, no. Yet they caused their problems, very troubling problems, to disappear quickly.

Take the Easy Way Out of Your Trap

We trap ourselves when we try to resolve personal problems using the unconscious problem-solving strategy that created the problem to begin with. The good news is that the Natural Brilliance model provides an ideal and easy way out.

To get out of a trap you must first realize you are in one. When you recognize you have come full circle—trying unsuccessfully to resolve a problem that only came back with a vengeance—stop the merry-go-round, and hop off. Many people feel distinctly frustrated or angry when they realize they are trapped in a dysfunctional cycle of problem-solving. Stop and release the emotions. Release the stress, and get back far enough to notice what is really happening. Releasing and noticing put you in a resourceful state of body and mind so that you can get distance from your emotions. You may be still stuck in the trap, but at least now you know you are holding the key to get out.

Next, do something different; respond and then witness the effects of your actions. Did you make things worse or better? Respond in an unusual way. Doing something creative, something zany, something unlike your typical response, gives you a reason to laugh and learn. Use any success in the direction of your goal to blaze a trail. Experiment, explore, discover.

The challenge is not releasing, noticing, responding, or witnessing. By now, those steps should be clear and fairly easy to perform. The big challenge remains—to define the real problem. Defining the real problem can be tricky because, if the problem you think is the problem is not the problem, then what is the real problem that you want to solve?

When you are willing to assume that the first problem definition you come up with is wrong, you are well on your way to success. Only then will you begin to explore. Do not assume you know what is going on. Be willing to enter the Zen "beginner's mind" and suspend there, oddly content to recognize you feel trapped, trapped by circumstances of your own design that you do not yet fully understand. Do not rush to solve the problem, but hover around it, releasing and noticing with curiosity, empathy, and humor.

This principle of staying with the problem rather than rushing to solve it leads to a process of creativity and problem-solving that I shall now describe. Using the Creative Problem-Solving process will ensure that you identify the problem in such a way that you can solve it.

Follow the Creative Problem-Solving Process

In this process, which I initially developed for Honeywell Corporation, the "problem" is simply the difference between the "present state" and the "desired outcome." You have a unique view of this difference. Someone else looking at where you are now and where you want to be will almost surely define and interpret the problem differently. Remember the riddle; the more definitions you come up with, the more scenarios you get.

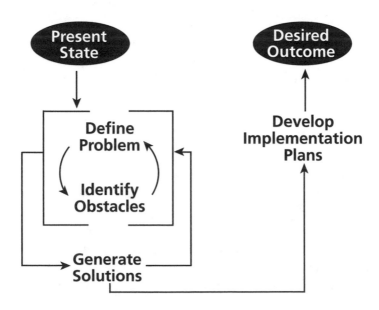

The first step in the process is to describe your present state and clearly define your desired result. Then you can take the difference between the two as your first description when you "define problem."

You will modify the definition of your problem as you consider obstacles between the present state and desired outcome. As each obstacle redefines the problem, the process chart shows a loop between "define problem" and "identify obstacles."

The clearer your definition of the problem, the more obvious your solution. Unfortunately, most people rush to get rid of their problems by prematurely grabbing the first and most obvious solution. I say *unfortunately* because the first solutions are the ones that occur to us based on our predominant problem-solving approach. Remember, it is your approach that traps you in your current problem.

Going back to the Creative Problem-Solving process chart, you see the loop between the step of "generate solutions" and the "define problem/ identify obstacles" loop. We have a loop because every solution we create redefines our problem—as in the riddle with the man at home wearing a mask. Every solution you implement carries its own load of attendant obstacles.

When the energy crisis of the 1970s hit, we waited in line at the gas pumps. The Detroit auto industry projected that energy efficient imported automobiles were going to be much more popular than the gas-guzzling American cars.

So the automakers decided to produce smaller cars. Smaller, lighter cars would sell. Problem solved, right? Well, partially. But look at the problem created for the steel industry. Detroit eliminated enormous amounts of steel from cars, virtually annihilating the steel industry that had depended on the automotive business. In Minnesota, we supplied taconite to the steel industry. Guess what happened here? The move to smaller cars all but destroyed the iron mining industry.

Perhaps you have heard the maxim:

> For want of a nail the shoe is lost, for want of a shoe the horse
> is lost, for want of a horse the rider is lost, for want of the rider
> the battle is lost, for want of the battle the kingdom is lost, and
> all for the want of a nail.
>
> George Herbert,
> *Poor Richard's Almanac*

I keep this age-old message framed above my desk: Take your time in defining your problem. Keep remembering there is a goal behind your goal. What is the real problem you want to solve?

In the Creative Problem-Solving process, I suggest that 80 percent of your problem-solving time might well be spent correctly defining the problem; the other 20 percent in generating a solution and implementing it. Think of this 80/20 ratio in relation to the Natural Brilliance model: 80 percent of the time is in releasing and noticing; 20 percent in responding and witnessing.

Spending such long and careful time on refining the problem may not be an easy approach for some people. The Creative Problem-Solving process requires a high tolerance for ambiguity and paradox. Again, think back to the riddle at the beginning of this chapter. Many people dash headlong on a straight line from problem to solution. Reality indicates a different approach.

Allow your thinking to meander into random, divergent, playful musings. Take time to ask lots of questions and test your hunches. Using the riddle as an inspiration, create many different scenarios to change the internal representations you clung to when you realized you had a problem.

Externalize the Problem

Several useful techniques can help you make the most of the Creative Problem-Solving process. These will heighten your divergent thinking, help you identify the correct problem, and aid you in generating solutions that work. The secret behind all the techniques is that they pull you out of feeling stuck. These techniques involve active, purposeful, inquisitive physical and mental movement. With them you shake up an otherwise static and stagnant view of the "problem-as-a-thing-causing-suffering" to reclaim your success.

In the Natural Brilliance retreat, we lead you to externalize the stuck state or problem you are working on by creating an analogy or metaphor for you to play with. We go on an outdoor experiential learning course, which we set up as a metaphor for your problem. You can create your own analogy any day of the week. Choose an important issue, one which puts you at risk if you do not solve it.

1) *Think of your own personal stuck state.*

One example might be that you feel you are stuck under the emotional domination of your parents. Let us pretend for sake of the example that whenever you talk with or visit your parents, at least one of them snoops into your personal life, which makes you angry. You are an adult, yet every time you communicate with them, you regress to age 11 and have to make excuses for not following their directives.

2) *Think of any significant event coming up soon.*

Let's say a friend asked you to do something you felt uncomfortable agreeing to. Because you felt uneasy telling your friend why, you acquiesced rather than possibly creating conflict. Imagine this situation as analogous to communicating with your parents. Assign your friend the role of your mom and/or dad.

3) *Create a full representation of your desired result.*

Imagine the way you want your life to be when you visit your parents. What kind of communication do you desire? How do you want to act? Are your parents your peers, friends, adults with common backgrounds, or what?

Consider your next get-together with the friend who made the request of you. What do you want? You might choose to express yourself directly and tell him or her "No."

4) *What internal or external obstacles might you face?*

Here is where you define the problem and identify obstacles following the Creative Problem-Solving process. Remember to keep playing with alternative explanations for why the problem stays in place. For example, consider that the problem exists because your parents have low self-esteem and will only feel good about themselves when they see your life has turned out perfectly. Or not. Play with it.

5) *Generate at least five to seven optional responses to move you in the direction of your goal.*

Think of getting together with your friend. You might take your friend a silly gift that means "Thanks, but no thanks." You could hand your friend a printed banner that says "Sorry, Charlie!" Who knows? Get creative! Set the goal as being able to disagree with or confront your friend appropriately if he or she tries to convince you to do something uncomfortable.

6) *Go into the event relaxed and alert. Respond in whatever ways you feel are appropriate at the time.*

Let go of your concern about doing well. After all, this is an analogous situation, not the real thing.

7) *After the event, witness the results of your actions.*

How did you handle yourself? What did you say to your friend? What is the moral of the story? What can that teach you about how to be, or not be, when you are with your parents?

Consider how the above technique allows you to disassociate from negative emotions and gain new perspectives. From such a resourceful mental and emotional place, you easily enter the witness mode, the source of most of your learning breakthroughs.

Enhance the Quality and Effectiveness of Solutions

The Natural Brilliance model suggests you *solve the way you solve problems.* It encourages creative and divergent thinking, feeling, and action and propels you to go beyond merely fixing the apparent problem. As a generative approach to solving problems, Natural Brilliance enables you to search for and find the solution to the way you have been trying to solve your problem.

In my work with individuals I have learned to listen for clues to paradoxical problems in people's descriptions of their problems. For example, when a person suggests "This is the only problem I have been unable to solve. If it weren't for this _____ problem (fill in smoking, weight, you name it), my life would be exactly as I want it to be."

Such a statement gives away that they are searching outside themselves for the "Ultra Solution," as Dr. Paul Watzlawick, the director of the Palo Alto Brief Therapy Clinic, describes it. A person seeking the end-all solution—the final answer that will cure all ills—will most likely miss the work that really needs to be done internally to solve the problem.

To follow a generative approach to problem solving and prevent the traps inherent within double binds, use the four steps of the Natural Brilliance model. In addition, do the specific behaviors of thinking and feeling that are presented under each of the three attitudes described in Chapter 8: *Put Natural Brilliance to Work for You*. To review, the attitudes include being *receptive, generative*, and *persistent*.

Being receptive means taking an attitude that you can safely explore areas that you had been afraid to consider. Discover what lies outside the boundaries and constraints you have accepted in the past.

Being generative means engaging in creative ways of thinking and feeling. You will need to bypass your inner critic to reach your creative childlike attitude, how you used to learn about the world before you started school. Roll up your sleeves and dip into a problem, without concern for "getting it right." Express yourself! Use your imagination with the abandonment of a child who finger paints with no worries of cleaning up the spatter.

Being persistent means establishing a clear vision of what you want for yourself now and in the future. It also means having the courage to believe you can create what you sincerely set your heart and mind to do.

Take the Right Path to Success

Let us review the secrets of success found in the combination of Natural Brilliance with Creative Problem-Solving. The five principles of Natural Brilliance discussed in Chapter 3 are:

> Principle 1: Tolerate ambiguity to realize your full potential.
> Principle 2: Make small adjustments slowly to accomplish your goal.
> Principle 3: Achieve a state of being by *being* not *doing*.
> Principle 4: Maintain an outcome orientation and increase choices.
> Principle 5: Change in generative ways for the best results.

One major addition is *Consider that your problem definition is wrong.* I put it this way because it is okay to proceed even though you may be pursuing the wrong problem. Witnessing the outcomes you produce will quickly give you feedback as to whether you are on the right track. If everything you have done increases oscillation, do something different—such as, redefine what you consider to be the problem.

Trust your mind to help you achieve your highest good in life. Know you are your own best therapist and educator. Following the Natural Brilliance model allows everything in your experience to give you feedback about how to proceed.

Remember my opening story in Chapter 1? I told you of my becoming faint during my icebreaker speech at Toastmasters. The following week, after numerous "mind control" techniques, I still had the same result. Why did I fail twice? What was wrong? What was my problem? Asking myself those questions about my failure, compounded my failure, because the only answers to them are excuses. Let's face it, I did what I did. Whatever I did, did not produce my desired results.

If my goal had been to "avoid failure," I failed big time. If my goal had been to "learn how to be the best public speaker I can be," then fainting was part of my learning, and therefore, part of my success. If instead I had asked "What did I learn?" or "How will this experience serve me to be a stronger, more accomplished speaker?" I would have discovered I learned a lot. Such questions bring out your witness and generate persistent learning in the direction of your goals. In the last part of the Toastmaster's example, I did the unthinkable. I broke the protocol for meetings by asking members to stay after. I asked for what I wanted, and I achieved it.

The power of effective goal-setting cannot be overestimated. If you set goals well, you greatly increase your chances of achieving them in record time.

Set Goals for Success

If you set a well-formed goal, you will enjoy an immediate payoff. A well-formed goal is the only kind that works. You can create effective goal statements by satisfying these five conditions:

1) *State your goal in the positive.* Your goal must positively specify what you want, not what you do not want. Instead of saying, "I want out of this boring job," state, "I apply my creative skills and energy to solve interesting problems in an exciting work environment."

2) *Focus on a goal within your control.* You cannot control how others feel. The goal "I want my office team to be happy" is not within your control. But the following is: "I do my part to create an office environment that supports my team's work."

3) *Create a goal that preserves what you value.* Craft a goal that maintains the things you value most in your life. If you have to give up too much to have a goal, it is unlikely you will seek it. For example, earning more money may take away from family time if it requires overtime or additional schooling. Make sure the trade-offs are worth it to you.

4) *Write your goal in the present tense.* Write your goal as if it has already manifested. Choose phrases such as "I am…" or "I choose…" You only need to know what it is you choose to create.

5) *Craft a measurable goal.* You must be able to know you have achieved your goal. To turn "I want to be happy" into a measurable goal, you must specify what happiness means to you. "I spend eight hours of quality time with my family each week" is a measurable goal.

Take a few minutes at your earliest convenience, if not right now, to think about your purpose for reading this book. Do the goals you have already established meet the conditions for effective goals? To be certain, write down your goals and check them. It will also be helpful to have clear goals when you head into the New Option Generator in Chapter 12.

Break Through in Business

The messages in this chapter are equally applicable for business. All of the stories and lessons of personal breakthrough can be viewed as metaphors in business. When you combine Natural Brilliance with

Creative Problem-Solving, you enter the role of educational consultant to yourself and performance consultant to your business.

As a consultant to organizations in both the public and private sectors, I have set up my role as an "inside-outsider." I act like an employee in establishing close interpersonal relationships with key employees and managers. At the same time, I act like the consultant in taking a long perspective on the organization. From an outside perspective, I fulfill my charge of offering straightforward, honest feedback to employees, managers, and directors, without fear of recrimination, such as losing my job.

An important part of my job as consultant, therapist, and educator is to plan for my own obsolescence; I am always working my way out of a job. I want my clients to learn the lessons they desire well enough that they can apply them on their own. They must develop self-sufficiency and the ability to learn from their experience. I help clients release what is not working, notice choices they have missed, generate their own positive responses, and witness the effects of their own behavior. If I work harder than my clients to achieve changes they want, then I am carrying them on my back to their success. When they arrive, they will be no more capable of maintaining their success than they were capable of achieving it.

With Natural Brilliance, organizations learn how to learn from their ongoing experience in business. No longer doomed to repeat the mistakes of the past, individuals who contribute move their companies into brilliant futures. When people express their genius by focusing it on resolving business problems, their emerging power impels the whole business toward its goals. A good leader is one who sees the potential all around and creates a work environment that engages the genius of every employee.

If you are a teacher or therapist, please consider the capacity for genius waiting to be revealed in your students or clients. When you see people as all that they can become, you activate a communication directly with their genius.

12

Generate Your Path To Personal Genius: The New Option Generator

The Natural Brilliance retreat activates the Natural Brilliance model so that all participants learn it cognitively, emotionally, and behaviorally. During the retreat, participants use seven exercises to bring up oscillations and move them past their internal limitations into the brilliance of their personal genius. The sequence of seven exercises forms a single system called the *New Option Generator*.

This chapter describes the New Option Generator so you can follow it on your own. Using it, you can resolve paradoxical problems and powerfully install the Natural Brilliance experiential learning model into your thinking, feeling, and acting. I saved the New Option Generator for last, because it assembles the whole of the Natural Brilliance model into one powerful system.

The New Option Generator relies on the Natural Brilliance model, Direct Learning, and the essential elements of Creative Problem-Solving. The process, when you follow it from start to finish, takes you through the following stages:

- *Release.* Stop oscillating, and prepare your body-mind for the changes you desire.
- *Identify the Continuum.* On what continuum are you currently oscillating?
- *Determine the Current Range of Choices.* How do they both support and limit you? Learn to recognize your typical stuck states. Experience them attached to the stop signs at each end of your current continuum of choices. Understand the feelings attracting you toward benefits you desire in the future and away from detriments you reject in your current behaviors.
- *Anchor States.* Clarify the benefits and detriments at each end of

the continuum and the powerful feelings that have been keeping
you stuck.

- *Collapse States.* Pop out the stop signs at each end of your continuum
  and stop oscillating.
- *Feel Positive Neutrality and Full of Choices.* Emerge with a pervasive
  physical and emotional sense of peace, almost as if you have
  facilitated a peaceful alliance of mutual respect, learning, and
  success between two cultures.
- *Make a Choice.* In accord with your personal power, decide what
  you want to create.
- *Take Action.* Respond with commitment in the direction of your
  desired goal.
- *Witness.* As you realize the outcomes of your natural learning state,
  choose to take the next steps to fulfill your desires.

To illustrate the New Option Generator and how it works for personal
transformation, I want to share a personal experience. A bit of background
on my problem will help set the stage.

During my thirties, I appeared dozens of times on local and national
television programs. Rather than feeling more capable with each show, I
felt progressively more uncomfortable in front of television cameras. I had
excellent studio skills from making audio programs, and I had mastered
the radio interview. But when it came to television, I got progressively
more stuck.

Part of my success on radio came from making eye contact with
the talk show host and building nonverbal rapport. But on TV, when the
camera went off the host, the host looked everywhere *except* at me, which
threw me off.

Associates assured me that I had performed well on TV talk shows,
but I *felt* like Mr. Stiff. After a decade of experiences, I knew I was getting
worse. At the same time, I held the belief that mastery in front of the
camera was critical for my continued success in the human development
field. So I put myself under a lot of pressure to do well.

On my fortieth birthday I set a goal. I decided I would do whatever
it took to finally master the video media. Within one week (small
coincidence, eh?) I received a call from a satellite-based self-improvement
network, asking me to develop and record 12 television shows on various
courses I had taught over the years. When I put down the phone, I started

oscillating. I became a walking yo-yo. Clearly, I had a goal and a great opportunity to achieve it. But, let me tell you, I wanted to run as fast as I possibly could in the opposite direction!

During the month after the invitation to script the TV shows, I busily developed the Natural Brilliance training protocols. For one of the exercises I took a group of participants to a ropes course to experiment on a set of outdoor experiential learning initiatives. I picked one event, known as the "Pamper Pole," as my personal challenge. To confront my fear, I set up conquering the pamper pole as a metaphor for starring in the TV shows. Whatever I did on the learning initiative would teach me how to perform well on TV.

When it was my turn to climb the 40-foot pole and stand without support on top of a wobbly disk bolted to the top, I knew what I wanted to achieve. Once harnessed and belayed with ropes, I scampered up the pole without hesitation or fear. As I took the final step to the top, my heart was pounding. I stood, arms outstretched, breathing in the magnificent view of the surroundings.

I felt as if my heart would explode. Then I realized, in the midst of my adrenaline rush, "*This is not fear I'm feeling—it's thrill and excitement.*" I drank in the realization that, of course I need to build skills, but I'm not afraid of being on TV. One day I will experience this same rush when I do a national TV appearance, and it will not be from fear. It will be from the thrill of having climbed to the top of such a magnificent vista.

The shows I created that autumn turned out to be the best television performance training course I could have wished for. I had an entire week in front of TV cameras recording over 28 hours of tape. I learned useful skills and realized that I had left my concerns about TV well behind me.

The following spring, we received a call from a producer at "CBS Up to the Minute News." To do a five-minute interview with me on PhotoReading, they needed to link me in Minneapolis to the hosts in the New York studio by satellite. In all the excitement I felt steady and cool.

On the evening of the interview my wife commented on how calm I had been all day. I did feel good. I was looking forward to doing the show. When I arrived at the CBS affiliate in Minneapolis, they led me into "Space Control," as they call it. I sat in the small room, barely bigger than my closet, staring into the lens of a camera. Behind me was a giant postcard of Minneapolis at dawn; in my ear an uncomfortable audio umbilicus to the New York studio.

When the satellite link went online, they could see and hear me in New York and I could hear them. After I joked about spinach in my teeth with the host, the producer said, "All right, gentlemen, thirty seconds." That's when it hit me.

All of a sudden my heart rate hit the high end of the aerobic zone. It felt like my necktie was flapping on my chest. I was sure they could see my neck throbbing in New York. Then, like magic, there I was on top of the pamper pole looking across the nation. *"This is not fear; this is the thrill of my career."* Just as fast as the thought appeared, my body flooded with energy. I felt the complete connection of mind, body, spirit linking with power and purpose.

The interview went flawlessly. The next morning, the phones at Learning Strategies Corporation started ringing. CBS called two days later to say they had received inquiries as well, which is unusual for them. The greatest accolade came when the producer invited me back for a story on Paraliminal programs.

More potent than any one experience in my story is the fact that every time I appear in the media, I add to my set of skills. I have opened the path of lifelong learning regarding presenting before the television media, and I witness continual growth in the direction of my professional goals.

Do the New Option Generator

Doing the seven exercises of the New Option Generator is designed to use your energy surrounding a paradoxical life issue to establish useful behaviors as strong and available resources. You can do it alone or have another person guide you through Exercises 2 and 3. You can modify the pace at which you do the steps.

If you are working with a partner who also wants to effect a change, you can take turns completing Exercises 1 through 3, then complete the Direct Learning in tandem or independently. Stop after each section of the exercise to discuss what you discovered with your partner.

With this Mind Map of the New Option Generator, you can follow the sequence:

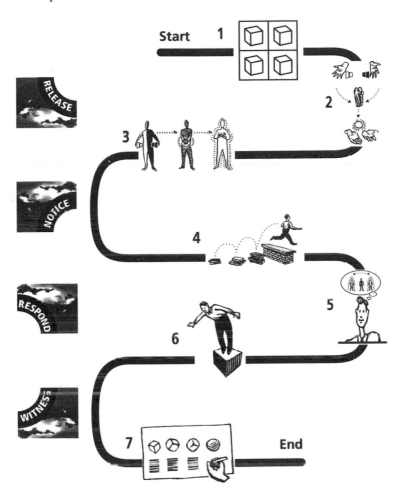

Exercise 1: Define the Problem Issue

A) Identify a life issue, or problem, you want to resolve. Ideally, use the issue you wrote about on the worksheet in Chapter 9.

B) Take four pieces of paper, of four different colors if you like, and in the center of each print the name of one of the four quadrants: *Present Negatives; Present Positives; Future Negatives; Future Positives.*

Present Negatives are problems, or *detriments,* you want to get away from or "eliminate" from your life. Wanting to stop doing and being these things may be the driving force for your wanting to change.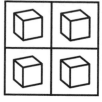

Present Positives are *benefits* you want to "keep," or not lose, even as you eliminate the present detriments to achieve what you desire.

Future Negatives are problems, or *detriments,* you want to "avoid" when you achieve what you desire.

Future Positives are *benefits* you want to "achieve" in making your desired change. Wanting to start doing and being these things may be the driver for your wanting to change.

C) Relax into a receptive, learning state of mind. Follow the directions for entering the resource level of relaxed alertness. In this relaxed state, think about each of the four quadrants. What experiences represent each quadrant? Explore your feelings and any images associated with each of the four quadrants.

When you are ready, open your eyes, but remain in a relaxed and creative state. Using colored pens, if you like, around each of the quadrant names, quickly write words and draw pictures that characterize each of the quadrants. Your words and pictures can express *being* and *doing*. Continue putting items on the four pages until you feel finished. If another item occurs to you later, add it to the appropriate page.

Option: Label each item with a code letter indicating the sensory modality that each word and each picture expresses— **V**isual, **A**uditory, **K**inesthetic, **O**lfactory, **G**ustatory. Beside each item, put the letter that corresponds to the sensation in your body when you think about that part of your life issue. For instance, under *Present Negatives,* I would have written about my TV challenge, *the show host looking away* – **V** and *feeling stiff* – **K**. Somebody who wants to slim down and has found that exercising works (if he would do it consistently) might write, "*Couch Potato!*" – **A/K**, because he calls himself that when he looks in the mirror and feels bad for not exercising. Or he might make a drawing of a slim waist – **V**. Noticing how many times you have written each letter can indicate how these detriments and benefits are affecting you.

D) Designate one hand to hold the *present* and the other to hold the *future*. An easy way to choose which is which is to say to yourself "On the one hand my future looks bright" and notice which hand you hold out as you gesture. The other hand is designated to hold the *present*.

Exercise 2: Integrate the Detriments

A) Looking at all the detriments you have put on your *present negatives* page, experience the negative things that have made you want to eliminate this issue from your life. Use your creative imagination to place all the *present negatives* into the "present" hand. Imagine all the consequences of the detriments, with all their associated punishments—as they look, sound, and feel.

Now imagine holding in your hand an object symbolic of all the present negatives you want to eliminate. As you imagine this symbolic object in your hand, notice what it looks like and feels like—its size, shape, weight, density, texture, temperature, color. Pay special attention to its surface. Is it angular or rounded, rough or smooth? Are there any sounds associated with this object? Imagine that you can feel it not only in this hand but also in this arm, shoulder, in this side of your body, this side of your face, chest, abdomen, pelvis, thigh, in this leg. Imagine that you have a line down the center of your body, dividing this side containing the issue from the other side of your body.

B) Looking at all the detriments you have put on your *future negatives* page, experience the negative things that you will want to avoid as you achieve your desire. Use your creative imagination to place all the *future negatives* into the "future" hand. Imagine all the consequences of the detriments, with all their associated punishments—as they would look, sound, and feel if they came to fruition.

Now imagine holding in your hand an object symbolic of all the future negatives you want to avoid. As you imagine this symbolic object in your hand, notice what it looks like and feels like—its size, shape, weight, density, texture, temperature, color. Pay special attention to its surface. Is it angular or rounded, rough or smooth? Are there any sounds associated with this object? Imagine that you can feel it not only in this hand but also in this arm, shoulder, in this side of your body, this side of your face, chest, abdomen, pelvis, thigh, in this leg. Imagine that you have a line down the center of your body, dividing this side containing the issue from the other side of your body.

C) Identify each side as different, separate, and present in the respective hand and the respective side of your body. Experience the extent of the no-win condition that has existed between these antagonists for so many years, with each side believing that it held the key to success and that the other side was wrong. *Realize also that each side has always had a single positive mission—to protect you so that you could live your life effectively.*

D) Invite a sense of the peacemaker into yourself. Imagine, like the Geneva Convention, a peace table, where these opposing forces communicate with each another. Invite a dialogue between the present negatives you want to eliminate and the future negatives you want to avoid, in which each side learns from the other to balance and harmonize your life.

E) At a rate determined by your ability to let go and integrate the learning of these previously opposed world views, integrate the sides of your body by bringing your hands together. As the palms of your hands press each other lightly, notice the felt shift throughout your hands, arms, face, body, and legs. Notice a new sensation and a new image, and feel a new resourceful symbolic object now resting in the cup of your hands.

Then, to complete the integration, cradle this new symbolic resource over the center of your chest, and with a deep inhale, breathe all of these resources into you. As you do, imagine all this learning from your life history, all the energy associated with this issue, now fully integrated and available to you, aligned for the purpose of helping you accomplish your highest good in life.

Exercise 3: Integrate the Benefits

In this part of the exercise you will imagine the polar opposites of the same issue in your respective hands. This time you will represent how each side has been operating successfully to 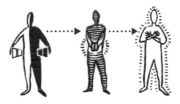 get you what you want in life; in other words, you will represent all the benefits. In each hand you will place the experience of behaviors associated with this issue in which *you acted appropriately, you liked your results, and you ended up with the feelings you wanted.* Look at the items on the two pages to evoke the sensations of the two quadrants.

Again, clearly identify each side as different, separate, and present in its respective side of your body and brain. Place the *present positives* where the present negatives had been; place the *future positives* where the future negatives had been. Then, bring your hands together. Here is the script for how to integrate the present and future positives:

A) Looking at all the benefits you have put on your *present positives* page, experience the positive things that you want to keep in place. Use your creative imagination to place all the *present positives* into the "present" hand. Imagine all the consequences of the benefits, with all their associated rewards—as they look, sound, and feel. Now imagine holding in your hand an object symbolic of all the present benefits you want to keep.

As you imagine this symbolic object in your hand, notice what it looks like and feels like; its size, shape, weight, density, texture, temperature, color. Pay special attention to the edges of it. Is it angular or rounded, rough or smooth? Are there any sounds associated with this object? Imagine that you can feel this object not only in this hand, but in this arm, shoulder, in this side of your body, this side of your face, chest, abdomen, pelvis, thigh, in this leg. Imagine that you have a line down the center of your body, dividing the side containing the issue from the other side of your body.

B) Looking at all the *benefits* you have put on your *future positives* page, experience the positive things you will achieve when you accomplish your desire. Use your creative imagination to place all the *future positives* into the "future" hand. Imagine all the consequences of the benefits, with all their associated rewards—as they look, sound, and feel when they come to fruition.

Now imagine holding in your hand an object symbolic of all the *future positives* you want to achieve. As you imagine this symbolic object in your hand, notice what it looks like and feels like—its size, shape, weight, density, texture, temperature, color. Pay special attention to its surface. Is it angular or rounded, rough or smooth? Are there any sounds associated with this object? Imagine that you can feel it not only in this hand but also in this arm, shoulder, in this side of your body, this side of your face, chest, abdomen, pelvis, thigh, in this leg. Imagine that you have a line down the center of your body, dividing this side containing the issue from the other side of your body.

C) Identify each side as different, separate, and present in the respective hand and the respective side of your body. Experience the extent of the no-win condition that has existed between the antagonists for so many years, with each side believing that it held the key to success and your believing that you could not have both. *Realize also that each side has always had a single positive mission—to compel you to live your life effectively.*

D) Invite a sense of the peacemaker into yourself. As at the Geneva Convention, imagine a peace table, where these opposing forces communicate with each another. Invite a dialogue between the present positives you want to keep and the future positives you want to achieve, in which each side learns from the other to balance and harmonize your life.

E) At a rate determined by your ability to let go and integrate the learning of these previously opposed world views, integrate the sides of your body by bringing your hands together. As the palms of your hands press each other lightly, notice the felt shift throughout your hands, arms, face, body, and legs. Notice a new sensation and a new image, and feel a new resourceful symbolic object in the cup of your hands.

Then, to complete the integration, cradle this new symbolic resource over the center of your chest, and with a deep inhale, breathe all of these resources into you. As you do so, imagine all this learning from your life history, all the energy associated with this issue, now fully integrated and available to you, aligned for the purpose of helping you accomplish your highest good in life.

Note: After doing Exercises 1, 2, and 3, a tremendous amount of learning continues to take place at a nonconscious level. Some people need to rest for a few minutes or take a nap before continuing. Others may need to sleep longer for a couple of nights. Some people report that they get "the munchies"—a need to eat some "brain food." At least, take a break and drink a glass of water.

Exercise 4: Engage Direct Learning

A) Select five books that offer knowledge and skills related to your life issue. Three of them should be directly related to the topic; two,  metaphorically or indirectly related. (Also see Chapter 10 on Direct Learning)

B) For each book, establish a clear purpose, get into state, and

PhotoRead. You can stay in state to PhotoRead all the books at once, or you can break state between books and do five separate PhotoReading sessions. In either case, I consider it essential that you affirm your specific statement of purpose before PhotoReading each book.

You can consider modifying your purpose statement slightly before each book to ensure your mind understands the relevance of each book to your overall outcome. For example, if your issue is overcoming procrastination to achieve success in business, you might choose books on decision-making, motivation, and time management. For one book you might say "I desire the information in this book to assist me in taking quick action on decisions." For the next you might say "I desire the information in this book to enhance my motivation and wise use of my time during the work day."

C) If you like, spend 5 to 15 minutes exploring each book consciously. Exploring gets the brain started on the process of linking your mind's new inner knowledge base with your body's responses to achieve your goal. Over the next several days and weeks, notice positive behavioral changes appearing spontaneously in your life.

Exercise 5: Simulate Future and Change History

A) Using your creative imagination, take yourself into the future and experience how the new choices and behaviors you desire operate in your life. Play "as if" you are experiencing a future situation and enjoy achieving the results you desire.

B) Continuing to play "as if," imagine the successful operation of these new patterns of thinking, feeling, and behaving in your present life circumstances (or in the recent past of no more than three months). As with all creative imagery, be sure to involve all your physical senses vividly. Include seeing, hearing, and feeling what it is like to enjoy being in the experience of your success.

C) Finally, imagine how your life would have been in the past, assuming all of these new choices had been fully available to you five years ago. Simulate fully that these new patterns are being used by you in this situation in your past and how you enjoy the success of accomplishing your desired results.

Consider briefly how your present life is different, given that you exercised all those choices five years ago.

Also consider how your future, five or ten years from now, is different, given all those choices were fully available to you five years ago.

Exercise 6: Take the Learning Challenge

During the Natural Brilliance retreat, participants go outdoors onto the "ropes course" to enter a physically and emotionally challenging learning opportunity. Here the participants experience a "high perceived risk, low actual risk" learning challenge.

For anyone outside the Natural Brilliance retreat, generally speaking, life delivers enough experiential challenge to activate what we have learned. For example, in this book I have referred to joining Toastmasters and being on TV as my ways to confront stuck states regarding public speaking. Do the thing that you fear most, where it is safe for you to fail. This gives you a scenario of "high perceived risk, low actual risk." To illustrate this step, I will describe the tasks we do in the Natural Brilliance course.

A) Select a challenge or learning initiative that brings up the oscillation associated with your life issue. Describe how the physical challenge—such as my experience on the pamper pole—represents a metaphor for your paradoxical life issue. Do your best to re-experience the full extent of the no-win situation in your body as you describe the metaphor.

B) With a partner, and if needed with a safety facilitator, plan your personal challenge.

C) Before beginning the initiative, release your need to control the outcome of the life issue. Release any unnecessary tension from your body. Increase your sensitivity to the world within and around you. Enter a curious, open state of mind and body so that you can notice whatever happens as you respond to the challenge of the initiative.

D) Afterward, debrief the experience with your partner. Describe your insights and the ways your body and mind responded to achieve the outcomes you produced. Explore how these insights can help you achieve the results you desire.

Exercise 7: Keep Track of Your Achievements

The Natural Brilliance model guides you to learn from experience and integrate your new skills and knowledge as you go. Experience always teaches most powerfully and honestly, but we do not always get the 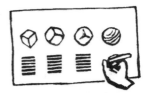 message consciously. Each day of the Natural Brilliance retreat, participants take time to examine what milestone they have reached in their experience. They receive feedback each day regarding whether or not they are living "on purpose."

You can assist the transfer of experiential learning into your awareness by consciously witnessing your achievements and keeping track of them. Here are some of the ways:

- Journal your achievements. Record the self-limiting beliefs you have released, and notice the choices you now perceive. Recognize the new responses you have been making and the learning you are witnessing.
- At work, notice how your choice of new options brings success.
- Meet weekly—even monthly—with a partner to integrate your life's experience and stay on purpose.
- Mind map what happened to you regarding this life. If you are not familiar with mind mapping, simply take notes on your experience so that you document a chronology of key events and highlight your personal responses.
- Commit to yourself or to your partner to exhibit your Natural Brilliance in all areas of your life as you continue to learn from

your experience and gain the skills you need for success.

- Dream, and interpret how your dreams apply to your achievements. Dreams can provide useful information about internal changes taking place. Dare to dream about the greater potential you can realize.
- Draw, sculpt, compose, write a poem, or dance to express your achievements.

Summary

Play with the New Option Generator to break through your limitations. Discover the ease of living in harmony with your life's purpose.

The universe says "*YES*" to you. What question will you ask? What goals will you seek? How much pleasure can you tolerate? How much joy do you want?

You know you can accomplish more once you have stopped oscillating. The New Option Generator aligns your internal and external energies. It ensures an effortless path to success in areas of life where you may have been stuck in the past. The more you play and explore, the more you will experience and learn. Learning is the surest way to release your genius and let your Natural Brilliance shine!

> I've noticed learning to trust my inner mind takes about six encounters. If I'm going to teach something in public, I like to have about six rehearsals with it before I feel comfortable. In teaching myself a foreign language, I found six exposures to it seemed to make the difference. Although I think a single exposure is enough for the mind to record it, it takes about six exposures or experiences before the trust in our ability to learn it will become strong.
>
> Peter Kline, Chairman of the Board
> Integra Learning Systems

13

Stay on Track

Congratulations on reconnecting with your Natural Brilliance. On your path to success, Natural Brilliance releases the fullness of your personal genius with each step you take. Along the way to achieving your goals, you will discover new capacities and reveal brilliant new strategies you never knew before. Your receptivity, generativity, and persistence will strengthen each day, giving you the power to venture well beyond your previous limitations.

Any journey outside of your comfort zone is not without its perils. I expect that your path will take you into uncharted territories. This chapter is written to give you some hint of what you may encounter along the way. As difficult as your path may become, take solace in knowing your Natural Brilliance can illuminate even the darkest places. Let me share my personal experience as example.

During my development of the Natural Brilliance course, I gathered 19 people from around the country to participate in a weekend workshop. Late Saturday night we were scheduled to go nightwalking. As I described in Chapter 5, nightwalking involves walking in the dark of a moonless night through the countryside.

After doing some exercises on how to walk with full awareness, we walked down a park road for ten minutes to get a feeling for the process. We donned our nightwalking hats, replete with a luminescent bead at the end of an 18-inch rod attached to the brim. The bead gives us a near focal point that promotes PhotoFocus for everything in the distance and around us. The 19 people followed me at a slow, steady walk, in succession about ten paces one behind the other. When we arrived at the trailhead for the nightwalking experience, I offered several final pointers about relaxation and trust.

I said, "If there are no questions, let's line up and do it! First person, follow me to the trailhead." With complete confidence I strode across a 75-foot clearing to the start of the two-mile forest trail. Suddenly I realized I was at the opening in the woods where the path began, but I absolutely could not see a blasted thing. The shock of being completely blind with nineteen people behind me caused my limbs to stiffen. With halting, jerky movements my feet groped for the trail in the abysmal blackness.

Instantly, 700 excuses raced through my mind on how to get out of this disaster. Forget the fact that this was the event most of the people had been waiting for; I could not see anything! This was not going to work!

Just as quickly as I had panicked, the calm inner voice of genius spoke, "Your brain can do this, Paul. Trust the process."

"Yes!" I thought. "Release. Notice the bead. Walk on."

Consciously I had no idea if I were walking straight toward a tree or into the thicket next to the path, but, miraculously, I moved in perfect rhythm and absolute balance. With each step my inner mind became more aware, more precise; my breathing, deeper and more relaxed. I witnessed a complete transformation from a tentative, halting, unsure step, to a long, confident, even stride.

After the successful nightwalking experience, stories from participants were wonderful, but no story was more profound to me than my own. I went from total oscillation to success almost instantly. Instant transformation from stuck state to heightened learning state is exactly what I offer you in this book. To test it, you must go on in your own life with a passion to learn and a commitment to succeed.

Most people will blame something else or someone else for their limitations and obstacles. If you lay blame, you are sure to lose power and stay stuck. If you choose to own your part in the process of getting stuck, you will increase power and propel yourself to success. When you fully accept that there are no failures, only outcomes, you banish the need to blame. Shame vanishes; ego and pride have no role. Focus the great talents you possess through the model of Natural Brilliance, and you will make the most of your life each day.

This chapter presents ways for you to stay on your path to success, even when you are blinded by limitations. Obstacles and limitations are built into the very design of our neurophysiology, as well as the culture in which we were raised. The most common of these limiting barriers were described in James Adams' book *Conceptual Blockbusting* and are shared in the sections of this chapter that follow. I invite you to overcome the limitations that may be blinding you to vast resources at your disposal. Use the ideas below to stay on track to success and accelerate your progress.

See What You Cannot See: Overcome Perceptual Barriers

Our sensory systems and brain are designed to work very quickly. The brain recognizes patterns. We tend to see what we expect to see and then focus narrowly on what we recognize. When you have difficulty isolating a problem, take these measures:

Use all of your sensory systems to explore your environment, inside and outside of you. Explore what is going on from various viewpoints, and notice more of the information that is available on the surface. As any one sensory system gets saturated and habituated, keep switching the way you are perceiving. Change your state and keep exploring. Become curious.

Feel the Fear: Overcome Emotional Blocks

You don't like to fail any more than I do. Most of us are taught early in life to minimize or avoid failure and maximize success. This leads to a low tolerance for ambiguity, a fear of failure, no appetite for chaos, and a compulsion to succeed quickly. Consequently, many of us find it easier to judge someone else's new ideas than to generate ideas on our own.

Develop the ability to relax and sleep on your problems. Generate ideas, all the better if they veer off track. They will lead you to access more of your imagination. As you gain facility in using your imagination, paradoxically, you will also develop the ability to distinguish reality from fantasy.

In my classes, I often hear adult students say, "Oh, I'm no good at puzzles." Step up to the challenge of problem-solving rather than giving up before you start. It is okay to feel strong dark emotions while you are learning something new. Fear, anger, and sadness are quite common in the classroom. If you repress them, they persist. If you feel them, you can move past the emotional wounding that first put them there.

On the other side of the wound waits a fantastically creative part of your personality that grew discouraged years ago. When you let your creative self out, you unleash enormous power to transform your life for the best.

Question It: Overcome Cultural Barriers

Part of the American culture, the part that grew out of our pioneer beginnings, emphasizes rules, taboos, logic, and respect for hierarchies and tradition. That rule-ridden part of our culture dismisses fantasy and reflection as a waste of time, playfulness as something only for children, and problem-solving as serious business in which humor has no place.

For Natural Brilliance we must revel in our feelings and our intuition. Celebrate pleasure and playfulness as the best rules of all. I encourage you to use meditation and humor, do more with less, and question traditional taboos for which no valid bases exist.

Tell Them How It Is: Overcome Environmental Obstacles

How many times have you told your peers that you are learning something new, like PhotoReading, only to hear them poo-poo your enthusiasm. Some of the most common derisions include: "You've got to be kidding" and "Yeah, sure. If it works for you, let me know; I'll test you."

Face it, lack of cooperation and trust is more common than support for new ideas. People who work in a team environment recognize the autocrat who only values his own ideas and rarely rewards anyone else's contributions.

What can be done? In the *Star Wars* film trilogy, apprentice Jedi knight, Luke Skywalker, vowed he would never join Darth Vader, even if Vader were his father. But, in the end, Luke did risk his life to find the good in the evil Darth Vader. Join the campaign to release the inner genius in those around you. Be patient and persistent with yourself and them.

When you witness others trying to put down your attempts for a better world, look for the fear that drives their knee-jerk behaviors. Realize we are all in this world together. Together we can find a way to resolve the problems that keep us and our organizations stuck.

Overcome Intellectual and Expressive Barriers

Is it possible to think too much? An article published in the *Washington Post* titled "Reasoned Choice Is Not Always Right" by Malcolm Gladwell says "Yes." The article summarized many studies from the field of cognitive psychology that showed rational thinking leads to decision-making we may later regret and that thinking too much can lead to choices that, by objective standards, are bad.

People tend to solve problems with inflexible or inadequate strategies based on too few facts or on inaccurate information. Using the processes outlined in Chapter 11: *Approach Paradoxical Problems with Creative Problem-Solving*, and Chapter 12: *Generate Your Path to Personal Genius: The New Option Generator*, you expand your repertoire of problem-solving skills and overcome the intellectual and expressive barriers to creativity, learning, and success.

Beware the Invisible Barrier

The most insidious of all the obstacles on your Natural Brilliance path to success is one that you cannot see, hear, or feel. This obstacle is one of the most phenomenal forces in human experience, yet the least recognized. Used correctly, this force has the power to restore a quadriplegic to health. Used incorrectly, it carries a death sentence. It is the power of hypnotic influence.

Earlier in this book I wrote of my introduction to human development technologies when I trained as a professional hypnotist. From the very beginning I recognized that the professional hypnotist knows things about directing the powers of mind that most people will never discover.

The three most important trance phenomena used by stage hypnotists are actually operating continuously to limit the quality of your life right now, but you probably do not know them. These phenomena include amnesia, hallucinating that something exists, and hallucinating that something does not exist. When you understand how these trances limit your life, you can break their hypnotic control over you and expand your choices almost immediately.

A former stage hypnotist originally trained me in hypnosis. Since then, I have studied the work of several stage hypnotists, including my friend Paul McKenna from England, the world's foremost hypnotic celebrity. The stage hypnotist's secret lies in directing your perceptions. Here's how.

Hypnotists gain your compliance with a set of instructions involving concentration and imagination. As you follow their instructions, the hypnotists bypass the critical faculty of your conscious mind. Then, they get your inner mind to wrap around a compelling idea using imagination and artfully crafted suggestion.

More than anything else, professional hypnotists understand that the mind will carry out any instruction it believes to be true. So they deliver their suggestions with enormous congruence and charismatic, authoritative, compelling belief. They give their subjects no opportunity to doubt or to interject any negating belief.

People in trance may be instructed that they have no memory of the number 5 or that they cannot remember their own name. Notice how similar those suggestions are to the self-limiting suggestions "I'm just no good with numbers" or "I am terrible with math" or "I've never been good with names; I'll never remember your name." Those negative statements about self make use of the same trance phenomenon that produces amnesia. Stop to consider the illogic of those statements; if we have perfect brains with an infinite memory storage capacity, why should we ever forget anything?

A trance subject will accept the suggestion that a person standing next to them cannot be seen. Even if the person stands in front of the subject, the subject has no ability to see the person. The person can speak and the subject hears but has no idea where the voice is coming from. Think of how we lose the keys we have just set down, as we busily tell ourselves "I can't believe this! I just set them down, and I can't find them anywhere!" We are inducing the phenomenon of negative hallucination.

Similarly, on the hypnotist's suggestion, a person in trance will believe spiders are crawling all over the chair and leap up in fright, frantically brushing off imaginary spiders. Have you ever picked a crawling tick off your leg, only to spend the next twenty minutes buggy as can be, imagining a multitude of insects crawling all over you? Imagining insects makes use of the same phenomenon the hypnotist uses—positive hallucination, imagining something is present that does not exist.

The good news is that these powers of hypnosis can be turned to your use. Use amnesia to forget the limitations of your past. Hallucinate that blocks have vanished that had been a part of your personality. Hallucinate that vast new powers of mind are now fully available to you. In other words, one way to instantly break the trance of a stage hypnotist or the self-limiting, self-negating trances that have controlled your life is to: *Tell yourself what you can do.*

The power of what people *can do* has been reverberating through the ages: "As a man thinketh in his heart, so is he." The philosopher Goethe put it: "Are you in earnest? Seize this very minute! What you can do or dream you can, begin it. Boldness has genius power and magic in it. Only engage and then the mind grows heated, begin it, and then the work will be completed." No more awesome power on earth exists than the power of people who believe in themselves.

Over the years, I have met people of faith who realize that the animating force in their lives is a power greater than they consciously wield—the power of God. However they may conceptualize this power, they hold that the limitations of the conscious mind are not the full extent of the possibilities in their life.

What I am referring to here is something better and more powerful than hypnosis. Hypnosis was the power used by schools and society to install many of the self-negating trances that run your life. You can instantly overpower the force of negative trances that have worked against you all your life. *Remember the truth about you.*

The truth about you is that you are a genius. You have magnificence beyond what anyone can ever predict about you. Each day that you believe in your great capacities, you will learn to release the limitations of your past, notice the new choices available to you, respond in creative ways to change your life for the better, and witness yourself learning how to create the results you desire.

You have been, and always will be, a natural, lifelong learner. For you—someone who chooses a high quality of life—the progressive realization of success always beckons you forward. You have Natural Brilliance, so let it shine on!

> **Stop; let go. Recognize what makes you marvelous, and get back more of what you focus on.**
>
> **Rex Steven Sikes**
> **Founder of IDEA Seminars**

14

Activate Your Natural Brilliance Daily

You cannot get stronger by joining a health club. You *can* get stronger by *working out* at a health club. Similarly, you cannot overcome stuck states and discover your genius by merely purchasing this book. You can activate your Natural Brilliance by *using* what you learn and giving your mind and body clear direction for success today.

By now, some powerful shifts in your life should have come with remarkable ease. In fact, if following the steps of the Natural Brilliance model ever becomes difficult, it is because you are getting too close to your breakthrough. Feelings of confusion serve as signs of learning, indicating that you are nearing new levels of awareness and positive new choices.

In the Natural Brilliance retreat I unleash a certain level of confusion when I ask participants to define the life issue they want to break through. As soon as their brain attempts to pin down a paradoxical problem, they begin to oscillate. I see the confusion instantly. Right on cue their hands go up. They start voicing doubts. They are not sure they know the *REAL* problem. Of course, they cannot fully know the *real* problem, and paradoxically, dwelling on understanding the *real* problem only throws the brain into greater oscillation.

The entire field of psychology has struggled with this seemingly irresolvable dilemma. Psychologists doing field research have vowed to use the scientific method to study the workings of the mind. We have an experimental paradigm in which the subject is studying the subject. The mind studying the mind is like looking at a Möbius strip, a continuous looped band with a half-twist, and trying to figure out where it starts and where it ends. The mind will always influence the outcome of its own experiment, creating an infinite recursivity.

As a facilitator, I can see the craziness of a person entering their own loop and looking for the beginning and the end. The participants cannot find the way out—at least not using the same training they used to create their stuck states. After a short time, their confusion leads some participants to feel enormous frustration. It is quite evident that the more desperately they want to rid themselves of their current problems, the more tenaciously the trap clings to them. They can babble endlessly about their problem, but talk is cheap. In my programs I evoke experience. *Talking about* experience is not *experience.*

Put your fingers into a Chinese finger puzzle and try as hard as you can to extract your fingers by pulling. You cannot. Try talking about how much you want to get rid of the trap. Your fingers still stay stuck. If you read this book and try to figure out your problem without doing the exercises I have offered, you have an even bigger problem than you bargained for. I am not there with you to facilitate your learning and evoke alternative responses.

TEST: If you are working hard at trying to make Natural Brilliance work for you, and you are getting no results, you are doing it wrong.

REMEDY: As I cannot evoke your experience, you will have to do it for me. Here is how. Go back to every section of this book you found difficult and every page you wanted to argue about or brush aside. In those sections are clues for your breakthrough. Follow every suggestion I offer, especially those you are convinced will not benefit you; do everything you are absolutely convinced you do not need to do; be everything you are convinced you do not have to be; feel all the feelings you claim you never feel. When you start oscillating—and I guarantee you will—when you hit your stuck state: Release! Then notice; then respond; then witness. That is all there is to it.

You may have heard the story of the successful businessman who was asked about the key to his success. He replied, "Success is the result of wise decisions. Wise decisions are the result of experience. Experience is the result of poor decisions."

Management expert Tom Peters wrote in his syndicated column "For Executives Only" the following gem: "Life is not about serenely walking down the middle of spick-and-span streets. It's about veering to and fro, bouncing off the guardrails, then overcorrecting. But you can't correct a course until you've taken to the road."

He continues with two provocative questions: "When will we learn to honor error? To understand that goofs are the only way to step forward, that really big goofs are the only way to leap forward?"

Natural Brilliance is a model for experiential learning, but, to have experience, we must be willing to venture out of the comfortable range of choices to which we have become accustomed. Living life fully offers the best way to have rich experiences. Life experience creates the most abundant form of learning opportunity. Get out beyond the stop signs and respond to life! Then witness the magnificent learning you gain in the process.

The subtitle of this book could be *When you meet your genius on the road, love it!* You will find evidence of your genius in your own behavior if you will simply witness it. When you find it, love it; reinforce it; affirm it; encourage it. Stuck states are evidence of past learning based on fear and repression. You create today and all your future days as you respond effectively, moment by moment, to purposeful choices based on what you want.

What do you want? That is the question. You will activate your Natural Brilliance today each time you actively, purposefully choose your response. I am not talking about instant manifestation of new relationships, income, business, a new house, or cars. I mean that you will create what you sincerely set your mind upon. As you drive fear out of your life and minimize the wild swings of oscillation, you increase your power to manifest your desires. Natural Brilliance shows you how.

My sincere desire is that you find your genius today and embrace it. Do all that you can today to live your life on purpose. Your good will surely come.

> **It takes courage to grow up and turn out to be who you really are...**
>
> **e.e. cummings**

Appendix: Advance Your Skills—
Tips for Applying the Natural Brilliance Model

Take New Routes to Release

Over the years of studying and practicing various forms of relaxation, I have found a number of helpful aids, tools that can facilitate the process of Release.

Training in contemplative prayer and meditation is a centuries-old path of wisdom in how to relax the body-mind to attune to higher levels of mental and physical functioning. These are primarily cognitive (thinking) and affective (feeling) approaches to relaxation. However, each system I have studied also emphasizes posture: prayerful poses, yogic asanas (postures), Zen sitting, and other techniques for stilling the body.

More active routes include various martial arts. Every session of Aikido, for example, begins with a contemplation of the teachers who have come before you. In the movements of Tai Chi, the mind and body move in a relaxed harmony free from mental or physical tension of any kind. In the Sufi tradition, the "whirling dervishes" enter an inner stillness and ecstatic release by twirling vigorously. Hatha yoga can be extremely vigorous physically, yet every element revolves around the principle of relaxing unnecessary physical and mental tension.

Aside from specific physical or mental disciplines, a number of modern electronic tools help the process of release. At the simplest level, an audio player with a recording of environmental sounds or relaxing music can do wonders. Machines that generate "white noise" soothe the mind and screen out unwanted sounds that may generate tension. Many dentists and oral surgeons offer patients a choice of recordings to distract the mind from the procedures.

Biofeedback machines are somewhat more sophisticated and expensive, yet they are marvelous tools for relaxation. These are electronic monitoring devices that give information about changes in the body or brain. The advantage to biofeedback training is that it makes subtle information obvious to you consciously, thereby letting you know if your changes in behavior are making a difference.

Electroencephalograph (EEG) biofeedback measures the electrical output of the brain. Data from an EEG tells you the frequency of the brain waves you produce. You can learn to willfully produce brain waves that are associated with states of deep meditation and learning.

I put on an EEG monitoring device and began PhotoReading. The computer immediately registered a decrease in conscious, analytical brain wave patterns and a corresponding rise in deep learning brain wave patterns. What an amazing thing to see graphically displayed on the computer screen. It convincingly demonstrated to me the power of training to get into state for learning.

One other useful tool I have experimented with extensively is known generically as a Sound and Light device. These machines give a light impulse through small lights in a set of goggles and a tone pulse through headphones. The sound and light pulses are delivered to the brain at certain frequencies, associated with different states of consciousness.

For example, the machine can help you get into a state of high creativity for visualization. It can help you enter an ideal state for learning, relaxation, even sleep. Simply punch in the program you want, put on the gear, and sit back.

Two Paraliminals, *10-Minute Supercharger* and *Deep Relaxation*, will help you develop states of relaxation and teach you how to quickly release any tensions from your body and mind. Using the *10-Minute Supercharger*, you will enter a physically relaxed state within two minutes of beginning the session. Then the program guides you through deep mental relaxation equivalent to a half-hour nap, without the hangover. R&R in ten minutes flat!

With *Deep Relaxation*, the longest of any Paraliminal session, you develop a profoundly relaxed state of body and mind. Along with the rejuvenating benefits of deep relaxation, the Paraliminal encourages optimism and control over your mind and body. One unique aspect of this session is that you have a choice at the end about whether you will awaken or not. If you want to slide from relaxation into deep sleep, you can. The session offers you the option of returning fully alert now or continuing the process of deep relaxation for as long as you desire.

By the way, going to sleep refreshed instead of bone-tired allows you to gain more benefit from your sleep. You will tend to awaken far more refreshed in the morning if you do a relaxation exercise before sleep.

Take New Routes to Notice

Practice opening your visual sense to notice useful information around you. In Chapter 5, I described aiming high when driving. I suggested walking with a soft gaze in crowds. These techniques help to open, strengthen, and balance your visual system, expanding its capabilities to serve you.

Another easy-to-find device tremendously increases noticing. It is the 3-D random-dot stereogram such as a "Magic Eye" poster. Seeing the pictures within a random-dot stereogram puts you into a state very similar to PhotoFocus. It requires that you diverge your eyes and simultaneously bring your focus to the poster. You can achieve the effect by crossing your eyes as well. First, see the image while diverging your eyes, then see it for the same length of time while crossing your eyes. The combination of playful exercise followed by relaxation can strengthen your visual system significantly.

Practice hearing more of the sounds around and within you. Play with the techniques and develop your auditory sense to a high level of acuity.

Digital audio recordings can be made with stereo microphones to record any portion of your day as you walk around. I have used a microphone near each ear, attached on either a hat or sunglasses. After your "walkabout" when you listen to the recording, you will hear information that you did not consciously perceive at the time.

Replaying an experience is similar to what happens when people lose their sense of sight. Suddenly, their hearing becomes amazingly acute to compensate for the loss of the visual sense. Equivalent to removing the flight blinders, the digital audio experiment awakens people from "tunnel listening." Listening to such a recording in stereo and surround sound is like pulling the ear plugs out of your neural circuits.

Another powerful technique, as simple as listening to a Paraliminal session, is "Paraliminal listening." This happens when you sit back and hear two voices speaking to you at the same time. It is like listening to several conversations at a party or restaurant at the same time. Known as the "cocktail party" effect (not to be confused with the cocktail weenie effect), the conscious mind attends the important information and weeds out the unnecessary. As there is too much information for the limited conscious mind to attend to, the nonconscious mind takes over.

A Minneapolis PhotoReading graduate named Mary had conducted university studies in fast listening twenty years before taking the PhotoReading course. Using a recorded lecture which she could speed up, she had students listen at faster and faster rates of speech. The experiment demonstrated that as long as students stayed relaxed and aware, they could listen to speech that was completely unintelligible to someone who might just happen to walk in and hear it.

Interestingly, she said that this worked only if the students "stayed in state," borrowing the term from the PhotoReading course. "If they ever broke state during the speeding up and lost what was being said," Mary explained, "they were unable to make sense of it again."

A surprising effect for Mary came about in her own visual processing with PhotoReading. Her ability to Super Read (an Activation technique in the PhotoReading whole mind system) was dramatically better than any other first-time PhotoReader in class. Could it be that fast listening twenty years earlier trained her in fast comprehension strategies for reading?

Here are some ways to sharpen noticing in the feeling dimension of your experience.

Think of yourself as spirit or soul, inhabiting the form of your physical body. The physical body is an energy field. (Research in subatomic physics will confirm this for you, in case you have doubts.) You express your thoughts—the product of spirit—in the world through your physical body.

Stuck states, at a subtle energetic level, can be perceived as improper or broken energy flows. Knowing where your stuck state exists in your physical body permits you to effectively redirect the energy.

Think of seven energy centers, defined from the Sanskrit term *chakra*, associated with the major clusters of nerve ganglia along the length of your nervous system. The first center is at the base of the spine. The second is at the sacral area. The third is in the solar plexus and the fourth near the physical heart center. The fifth is at the throat, the sixth on the forehead between the eyebrows, and the seventh at the crown of the head.

In the early work with resolving paradoxical problems, my partner Mark Kinnich and I researched the yogic and Jungian psychological issues or functions associated with the seven major chakras. When a person has a stuck state regarding the behavioral continuum of giving and receiving love, for example, it is primarily associated with the fourth chakra. Resolving this issue can be assisted by identifying and balancing the energies flowing through the fourth chakra.

To find out more about the chakra energy system and its connection to psychological issues, I recommend two books, *Yoga and Psychotherapy*, by Swami Rama, Rudolf Ballentine, and Swami Ajaya, and *Hands of Light*, by Barbara Brenan.

Strengthen the Body-Mind Connection: Go into State

Each morning I begin my day with a series of movement exercises. These are designed to increase flexibility, invigorate the body, strengthen and energize the nervous system, deepen breathing, and clear the mind. The specific exercises used are drawn from several disciplines including hatha yoga, Tai Chi, Mentastics (Dr. Milton Traeger), Awareness Through Movement (Dr. Moshe Feldenkrais), Brain Gym/Edu-K (Dr. Paul Dennison), and The Egoscue Method of Health through Motion (Pete Egoscue).

People interested in developing their Natural Brilliance are well advised to use physical awareness and exercise as an integral part of their daily routines. A common misconception is that life degenerates until death. This means that aging opposes vitality. Yet experience shows that proper breathing, diet, exercise, and attitude lead to good health and vitality at any age.

The ancient Chinese practice of Qigong has been renown to enhance the body-mind connection. *Spring Forest Qigong,* a complete self-study course by Master Chunyi Lin that we publish, describes it as an effective set of breathing, movement, and concentration exercises. The simple practices quickly remove energy blockages and increase the flow of vital energy to the body and brain. Students of Spring Forest Qigong achieve remarkable health benefits and enjoy increased mental clarity.

Assume Useful Postures

Like Qigong, physical or hatha yoga has developed over the centuries to arouse the latent energy within by practice and perfection of asanas (postures) and pranayama (breath control).

There are two kinds of postures, those for meditation and those for physical well-being. In all the postures suitable for breathing, concentration, and meditation, the emphasis is placed on keeping the head, neck, and trunk erect. This results in a steady and comfortable posture with minimal production of carbon dioxide, thus slowing down the activity of the heart and lungs. The mind is less disturbed by the body and can be directed to concentration.

Other postures, which aim at physical well-being, control specific muscles and nerves in the body and have specific therapeutic effects. Get expert coaching on morning exercise routines, then experiment with each for a week or two. The right sequence will wake up your body-mind in a gentle and effective way.

The hybrid series of joints and gland exercises, tai chi movements, and postures flow together in a 20-minute sequence. This sequence allows me to roll out of bed, flop on the floor, and begin with very low impact movements. It creates a perfect start in my day. I find my routine essential to maintain a high level of personal power during challenging days of teaching, public appearances, and creative writing.

The exercises stimulate joints and glands from head to toe, releasing the necessary biochemistry for flexibility and movement throughout the skeletal and muscular systems. They also increase the depth and capacity of the breath, a prerequisite for relaxed alertness. Finally, and perhaps most importantly, they strengthen the nervous system by increasing its capacity to process information and respond in the world.

Each day at 11:30 a.m. in the Learning Strategies Corporation offices, we invite our employees to participate in a 30-minute Spring Forest Qigong practice session. Guided by Master Lin's recordings, the movements and breathing revitalize the body, calm the emotions, and clear the mind. Those who participate can recognize how the physical and mental health benefits spill out into all areas of their lives.

The entire Natural Brilliance approach to personal power hinges on cognitive, emotional, and behavioral flexibility. Any strengthening of the body-mind connection ultimately makes power available to fuel experiential learning, choice, and successful action. To this end, I encourage you to follow a path of physical exercise.

Aerobic exercise is important for cardiovascular-vascular health, and I make a point to work out at least three days a week. Yet, physical well-being is just one part of the point I am making here. I am advocating a set of physical exercises, which when taken together, contribute advantages to overall well-being that cannot be achieved with aerobics alone. An approach like the one suggested above will move deeply into your cognitive and emotional well-being as well, where the real payback comes. Any time you spend in such disciplined physical practices will reap many levels of reward to you. Imagine what great feelings you will generate each day that you strengthen yourself in naturally brilliant ways.

After doing a sequence of movements, it is recommended that you lie down briefly to relax the body and mind, then sit in a meditative posture. From this posture, alternate nostril breathing can be performed leading into a time of meditation. I describe alternate nostril breathing in the next section.

You should feel free to use any form of meditation, contemplative prayer, or mind programming techniques that suit your lifestyle and personality.

Breathe

In the yoga tradition, after mastery of postures comes the technique of pranayama. The Sanskrit word *pranayama* can be divided into the words *prana* and *yama*, meaning breath control. Pranayama can also be interpreted as *prana* and *ayama*, meaning expansive, rising, or extensive breath. So pranayama can be understood to be the science whereby the flow of the breath is made more extensive and expansive and this flow is brought under control.

The word *prana* is composed of two words, *pra* and *na*. *Pra* means *first unit* and *na* means *energy*. Described by yoga philosophy, this first unit of energy is in its atomic aspect in man, and the universe is its expansion. This means that the underlying energy in both humans and universe is prana. Prana can be thought of as the sum total of all energy that is manifested in humans and the universe. The ancient traditions of yoga science and philosophy hold that all sensations, all thinking, feeling, and knowing are possible only because of prana.

The science of pranayama is intimately connected with the functions of the autonomic nervous system, and its techniques are aimed at bringing under conscious control the functions of the autonomous system, which are normally considered involuntary. Here is how the Himalayan Institute of Yoga Science and Philosophy describes it:

> Breath is an external manifestation of the force of prana. Breath is the flywheel that regulates the entire machine of the body. Just as the control of the flywheel of an engine controls all other mechanisms in it, so the control of the external breath leads to control of the gross and subtle, physical and mental aspects of our life machine. A comprehensive knowledge of Pranayama is of paramount importance in the raja yoga (royal path of yoga) tradition.

Many types of pranayama exercises exist, each for a specific purpose. Yoga teachers claim pranayama should be practiced only under the guidance of a guru or competent teacher. One breathing exercise that may be practiced by everyone without any danger is called "Channel Purification" which purifies the subtle energy channels. This exercise should be done at least twice a day—in the morning and in the evening. In the morning the exercise is done in the following manner:

1) Sit in a calm, quiet, and airy place in an easy and steady posture.

2) Keep the head, neck, and trunk straight and the body still.

3) The right hand is brought up to the nose, the index finger and middle finger being folded so that the right thumb can be used to close the right nostril and the ring finger can be used to close the left nostril.

4) Exhale completely through the left nostril, the right nostril being closed with the right thumb. The exhalation should be slow, controlled, and free from exertion and jerks.

5) At the end of the exhalation, close the left nostril with the ring finger, open the right nostril slowly and completely. Inhalation and exhalation should be of equal duration.

6) Repeat this cycle of exhalation with the left nostril and

inhalation with the right nostril two more times.

7) At the end of the third inhalation through the right nostril, exhale completely through the same nostril, still keeping the left nostril closed with the ring finger.

8) At the end of the exhalation, close the right nostril with the thumb and inhale through the left nostril.

9) Repeat two more times the cycle of exhalation through the right nostril and inhalation through the left nostril. This completes the exercise.

10) The exercise in the morning consists of:

a) Three cycles of exhalation through the left nostril and inhalation through the right nostril; followed by

(b) Three cycles of exhalation through the right nostril and inhalation through the left nostril.

11) In the evening the exercise consists of:

(a) Three cycles of exhalation through the right nostril and inhalation through the left nostril; followed by

(b) Three cycles of exhalation through the left nostril and inhalation through the right nostril.

You should be careful to see that inhalation and exhalation are of equal duration. Inhalation and exhalation should be slow, controlled, and free from jerks and any sense of exertion. With practice, you can gradually lengthen the duration of your inhalation and exhalation.

Achieve Goals without Self-Sabotage

Many clients have described their subconscious as a grand saboteur of their goals and best-laid plans. I have devoted a considerable amount of professional curiosity to that statement.

Most of our so-called self-sabotage is basically internal dialogue. When you desire to accomplish a goal, you can be completely derailed by simply inserting an analytical, fearful, or self-critical internal dialogue in the midst of taking action. Imagine focusing on making a golf shot and smoothly following through with your stroke. Then imagine at the height of your backstroke thinking, "Now make sure you stay away from that water hazard!" Your stroke falls apart, and the likelihood of your ball going into the water increases because you directed your attention to the water. We do not sabotage ourselves maliciously. The fearful, limited conscious mind is trying to help. Like a backseat driver, it does its best to make sure everything works out.

To eliminate self-sabotage, the *Automatic Pilot* Paraliminal trains you to be clear about what you want. This session asks you to form a goal that is stated in positive terms, within your control to achieve, beneficial in all ways, measurable, and worthwhile. When you have a clear goal, the Paraliminal leads you to wire-in the necessary behaviors for its accomplishment.

Using full sensory mental rehearsal, you imagine accomplishing the goal up to 21 times in seven seconds. The visualizations occur in a numerical progression known as the Fibonacci number series. The effect trains the brain to recognize what you want, so that when it is time to perform, you can go on automatic pilot, omitting the internal dialogue.

I always encourage my clients to reframe their view of the inner mind. Think of the inner mind as an ally not a saboteur. From years of field research, I have determined that if your subconscious has prevented you from succeeding, it is only because it knew no other way to help you. Your inner mind wants you to succeed and achieve inner peace.

Dream Your Way to Success: Activate Your Natural Brilliance

Dreaming may be the ideal way to activate your Natural Brilliance. Almost without conscious effort you can gain the advantage of having your brain work through the night to help you succeed. Because dreaming requires a minimum of conscious input, you eliminate the limitations and complications of analytical problem-solving. The inner mind can review information, work through problems, and present solutions to you when you awaken.

Everything you experience during the day is processed by the mind. Information that is not processed consciously is often reviewed and processed unconsciously during sleep. Dreams often reveal the mind's work at making sense of our experiences.

Dr. Norman F. Dixon in his book *Preconscious Processing* describes the Poetzl effect. In 1917, a cognitive researcher named Poetzl discovered that information presented subliminally is symbolically transformed and shows up as dream imagery at night.

Dr. Stephen LaBerge of the Stanford Sleep Research Laboratory wrote in his book *Lucid Dreaming*: "With the universe of experience thus open to you, if you must sleep through a third of your life, as it seems you must, are you willing to sleep through your dreams too?" His position is that learning to access your dreaming mind gives you a vast universe of human development opportunities. Every night you can use the gifts your dreaming mind offers you.

Before going to sleep at night, you can program your mind to get the maximum benefit from dreaming. Sitting on the edge of your bed, simply enter an accelerative learning state using the standard procedure described in Chapter 4 of this book. Take only a minute or two at the most to go into state. Then, program your mind to dream about the books you have PhotoRead that day and to remember the dream upon awakening.

After noticing your dreams each morning for a few days, you will get a feeling for the subtle and symbolic communication from your inner mind. Do not worry about making sense of everything you dream. Not all dreams are intended to make sense consciously.

Then, take the next step and play with problem-solving in your dreams. Program your mind to solve specific problems. If you divide the steps of the Natural Brilliance model, one night you could program your mind to release, the next night to notice, and so on.

Select and PhotoRead several books on the subject that will help you resolve your problem, as you do in Direct Learning. Then, invite your mind to put together the essential knowledge and reveal to you the direction you should follow to accomplish your goals. When you awaken, make mind map notes of your dreams. Often, the story line of your dream is a metaphor, a symbolic representation of what you can do to solve the problem you face. Examine your mind maps to reveal the insight your inner mind has to offer.

Review Your Day

You can believe that you can create today to be better than yesterday. When you take action on this belief, witness the results. You will develop a mind set for continuous improvement in your life.

Any incremental shift for the better moves you in the direction of your goals. The fastest way to gain shifts in behavior is to review your day each evening before sleep and offer nurturing self-talk from a place of witness. You mentally review your day while being aware of your purpose.

How did you do today? Is your *doing* consistent with the purpose of your *being*? If so, celebrate! If not, witness that discrepancy and gain internal support to achieve your purpose. Visualize the situations where you feel you could improve. Think of what you would do in the future if a similar situation arose. In this way you mentally rehearse success for the future.

The *New History Generator* Paraliminal can be valuable for rehearsing success. Session B teaches you the entire mental review process in a relaxing pleasant way.

Another tool I have used in training is called the MotivAider. It is a personal timer, the size of a paging device, that vibrates briefly at the time interval you set. The vibration reminds you of something you have determined will support you in your personal or professional development. You can choose to be reminded once every 24 hours down to as often as once a minute. This pocket buzzer alerts you to keep your purpose or goal at the forefront of your consciousness.

You can use the MotivAider to experience each of the four steps of Natural Brilliance throughout the day. For example, one day use it to release tensions or stresses in the body. Another day, remind yourself to release and notice something new in your surroundings. On yet another day use it to respond with behaviors or access highly empowered states when the MotivAider signals you. In these ways using a MotivAider reminds you to witness your life experience and stay on track to your goals, brilliantly.

Release the fullness of your personal genius with each step you take. Along the way to achieving your goals, brilliant new strategies will be revealed. You discover new capacities within that give you the power to venture well beyond previous limitations.

Bibliography

Adams, James L. *Conceptual Blockbusting: A Guide to Better Ideas*. Reading, MA: Addison/Wesley, 1986.

Andreas, Connirae. *Core Transformations: Reaching the Wellspring Within.* Moab, UT: Real People Press, 1994.

Bates, C. *Pigs Eat Wolves*. St. Paul, MN: Yes International Publishers, 1991.

Barbur, J.L., Watson, J.D.G.; and Frackowiak, R.S.J. "Conscious Visual Perception without V1." *Brain*, Oxford University Press, 1993.

Bennett, J. Michael. *Four Powers for Greatness Personal Learning Course.* Wayzata, MN: Learning Strategies Corporation, 1998.

Brennan, Barbara Ann. *Hands of Light: A Guide to Healing Through the Human Energy Field*. New York: Bantam Books, 1987.

Buzan, Tony. *The Mind Map Book*. New York: Penguin Books, 1994.

Carson, Richard. *Taming Your Gremlin*. New York: Harper & Row, 1983.

Castenada, Carlos. *The Teachings of Don Juan: Yaqui Way of Knowledge.* Berkeley, CA: University of California Press, 1968.

Campbell, Don G. *The Mozart Effect: Tapping the Power of Music to Heal the Body, Strengthen the Mind, and Unlock the Creative Spirit*. NY: Avon Books, 1997.

Covey, Stephen. *Seven Habits of Highly Effective People*. New York: Simon & Schuster, Inc., 1989.

Csikszentmihalyi, M. *Finding Flow: The Psychology of Engagement with Everyday Life*. NY: BasicBooks, 1997.

Cudney, M., and Hardy, R. *Self-Defeating Behaviors*. New York: HarperCollins Publishers, 1991.

Davis, Ronald D. *The Gift of Dyslexia*. Burlingame, CA: Ability Workshop Press, 1994.

Dennison, Gail E., Dennison, Paul E., and Teplitz, Jerry V. *Brain Gym for Business: Instant Brain Boosters for On-the-Job Success*. Ventura, CA: Edu-Kinesthetics, Inc., 1995.

DePorter, Bobbi. *Quantum Business: Achieving Success Through Quantum Learning.* New York: Dell Publishing, 1997.

Dixon, Norman F. *Preconscious Processing.* Chichester, NY: Wiley, 1981.

Dixon, Norman F. *Subliminal Perception: The Nature of a Controversy.* London, NY: McGraw-Hill, 1971.

Gardner, Howard. *Multiple Intelligences: The Theory in Practice.* New York: HarperCollins Publishers, Inc., 1993.

Gelb, Michael J. *Lessons From the Art of Juggling: How to Achieve Your Full Potential in Business, Learning and Life.* New York: Harmony Books, 1994.

Gordon, F. Noah. *Magical Classroom: Creating Effective, Brain-friendly Environments for Learning.* Tucson, Arizona: Zephyr Press, 1995.

Grinder, Michael. *Righting the Educational Conveyor Belt.* Portland, OR: Metamorphous Press, 1991.

Harman, Willis, and Rheingold, Howard. *Higher Creativity; Liberating the Unconscious for Breakthrough Insights.* Los Angeles, CA: Jeremy P. Tarcher, Inc., 1984.

Hunt, D. Trinidad. *Learning To Learn: Maximizing Your Performance Potential.* Kaneohe, HI: Elan Enterprises, 1991.

Hunt, D. Trinidad. *Remember to Remember Who You Are.* Kaneohe, HI: Elan Enterprises, 1992.

Hunt, D. Trinidad. *The Operator's Manual for Planet Earth.* New York: Hyperion Press, 1996.

Kandel, Eric R., Schwartz, James H., and Jessell, Thomas M. *Essentials of Neural Science and Behavior.* Norwalk, CT: Appleton and Lange, 1995.

Kelder, Peter. *Ancient Secret of the Fountain of Youth.* Gig Harbor, WA: Harbor Press, 1989.

Kermani, Kai. *Autogenic Training.* London, England: Thorsons, 1992.

Keyes, M.F. *Emotions and the Enneagram: Working Through Your Shadow Life Script.* Muir Beach, CA: Molysdatur Publications, 1992.

Kline, Peter. *The Everyday Genius: Restoring Children's Natural Joy of Learning—And Yours Too.* Arlington, VA: Great Ocean Publishers, Inc., 1988.

Kosko, Bart. *Fuzzy Thinking: The New Science of Fuzzy Logic.* New York: Hyperion, 1993.

Jensen, Eric. *Completing the Puzzle: The Brain-Based Approach.* San Diego, CA: Turning Point Publishing, 1996.

Jensen, Eric. *The Learning Brain.* San Diego, CA: Turning Point Publishing, 1994.

LeDoux, Joseph. *The Emotional Brain: The Mysterious Underpinnings of Emotional Life.* NY: Simon & Schuster, 1996.

Lee, Scout. *The Excellence Principle.* Portland, OR: Metamorphous Press, 1990.

Levinson, Steve, and Pete C. Greider. *Following Through: A Revolutionary New Model for Finishing Whatever You Start.* NY: Kensington Publishing Corp., 1998.

Lewicki, P., Hill, T., and Czyzewaska, M. "Nonconscious Acquisition of Information." *American Psychologist*: American Psychological Association, Inc., 1992.

Mattimore, Bryan. *99% Inspiration: Tips, Tales, and Techniques for Liberating Your Business Creativity.* New York: Amacom, 1994.

McKenna, Paul. *The Hypnotic World of Paul McKenna.* London: Faber and Faber Limited, 1993.

Michaels, R.E. *Facticity.* Seattle, WA: Facticity Trainings, 1991.

Michaels, R.E. *Lions In Wait: A Road to Personal Courage.* Seattle, WA: Facticity Trainings, 1993.

Miller, William A. *Make Friends with Your Shadow: How to Accept and Use Positively the Negative Side of Your Personality.* Minneapolis, MN: Augsburg Publishing House, 1981.

Miller, William A. *Your Golden Shadow.* New York: Harper & Row, 1989.

Minkoff, Robert A. "Searching for the Healing Tale." *Storytelling.* Jonesborough, TN: National Storytelling Association, 1995.

Montessori, Mario, Jr. *Education for Human Development: Understanding Montessori.* New York: Schocken Books, 1976.

Perkins, David. *Outsmarting IQ: The Emerging Science of Learnable Intelligence.* New York: Free Press, Simon & Schuster, 1995.

Pert, Candace B. *Molecules of Emotion: Why You Feel the Way You Feel.* New York: Scribner, 1997.

Promislow, Sharon. *The Top 10 Stress Releasers: Simple, effective self care to re-educate your reaction to stress...from the inside out!* Vancouver, British Columbia: Kinetic Publishing Corporation, 1994.

Rama, Swami. *Yoga and Psychotherapy: the Evolution of Consciousness.* Prospect Heights, IL: Himalayan International Institute of Yoga Science and Philosophy, 1973.

Ramachandran, F.S., and Sandra Blakeslee. *Phantoms In The Brain: Probing the Mysteries of the Human Mind.* New York: Morrow, 1998.

Restak, Richard M., M.D. *The Modular Brain*. New York: Touchstone, 1995.

Robbins, Anthony. *Awaken the Giant Within: How to Take Immediate Control of Your Mental, Emotional, Physical and Financial Destiny*: New York: Simon & Schuster, 1992

Russell, Peter. *The White Hole In Time: Our Future Evolution and the Meaning of Now.* New York: HarperCollins, 1992.

Scheele, Paul. *PhotoReading*. Minneapolis, MN: Learning Strategies Corporation, 1993.

Scheele, Paul. *PhotoReading Personal Learning Course*. Minneapolis, MN: Learning Strategies Corporation, 1995.

Scheele, Paul. *Natural Brilliance Personal Learning Course*. Minneapolis, MN: Learning Strategies Corporation, 1997.

Seigel, Robert Simon. *Six Seconds to True Calm*. Santa Monica, CA: Little Sun Books, 1995.

Seligman, Martin E.P. *Learned Optimism*. New York: Alfred A. Knopf, Inc., 1990.

Smith, Frank. *Reading Without Nonsense (2nd Edition)*. New York: Teachers College Press, 1985.

Tomatis, Alfred. *The Conscious Ear.* Barrytown, New York: Station Hill Press, Inc., 1990.

von Oech, Roger. *A Kick In The Seat Of The Pants.* New York: Harper & Row, Publishers, Inc., 1986.

von Oech, Roger. *A Whack On The Side Of The Head*. New York: Warner Books, Inc., 1983.

Watzlawick, Paul. *The Language of Change*. New York: Basic Books, 1978.

Watzlawick, Paul. *Ultra-Solutions: How to Fail Most Successfully*. New York: W.W. Norton and Company, Inc., 1988

Williams, Frank. *A Total Creativity Program for Individualizing and Humanizing the Learning Process*. Englewood Cliffs, NJ: Educational Technology Publications, 1972.

Ward, Christine, and Daley, Jan. *Learning to Learn: Strategies for Accelerating Learning and Boosting Performance*. Christchurch, New Zealand: BCP Print, 1993.

Wolinsky, Stephen. *Trances People Live: Healing Approaches in Quantum Psychology*. Falls Village, CT: The Bramble Company, 1991.

Zink, N., and Parks, S., "Nightwalking: Exploring the Dark with Peripheral Vision." *Whole Earth Review:* Fall 1991.

Index

Tools for Lifelong Learning

We offer what we believe to be the finest programs, seminars, and retreats in self-improvement, education, and health to help you maximize your potential. All of our programs come with success coaching as well as a money-back satisfaction guarantee.

Natural Brilliance

Paul Scheele will guide you through using the Natural Brilliance model to help you achieve a breakthrough in your life. The audio program features six remarkable Paraliminal sessions and six instructional sessions.

This *Natural Brilliance* personal learning course will help you automatically use the Natural Brilliance model in all areas of your life. The audio program includes:

Session 1: *Reclaiming Your Natural Brilliance*
- Four Steps of Natural Brilliance
- Optimum Performance Breakthrough
- How to Get the Most Benefit
- Understanding Stuck States
- Resolve Problems
- Three Attitudes of Natural Brilliance
- Diagnose Your Stuck States

Session 2: *Release*
- Release from the Tug-of-War Between the "Model of Success" and the "Model of Failure"
- Venture Beyond the Stop Signs in Your Life
- Instant Relaxation
- Paraliminal session: *Explore Life Beyond Stop Signs*

Session 3: *Notice*
- How We Create Oscillation
- The Optimum Learning State
- Increase Your Sensory Acuity
- Notice New Choices
- Overcome the Invisible Barrier
- Develop Intuition
- Paraliminal session: *Give Yourself a New Range of Choices*

Session 4: *Respond*
- Take Action
- Face Your Fears with Infinite Strength
- Trial and Feedback to Success
- Persistent Power
- Paraliminal session: *Unleash New Power to Respond*

Session 5: *Witness*
- The Oasis of Safety
- How to Learn Best
- Achieve a Witness Perspective
- Conquer Fears and Shadows
- Live on Purpose
- Paraliminal session: *Create Your Desired Future*

Session 6: *Natural Brilliance Generator*
Two Paraliminal sessions: *Using the "Model of Success" at Will*
(*retreat - self-study - book*)

PhotoReading

You learned about PhotoReading in Chapter 10 of *Natural Brilliance*. PhotoReading is a whole mind approach to read with speed, comprehension, and enjoyment. It features the technique of PhotoReading at 25,000 words a minute. Beginning PhotoReaders can have full comprehension of materials in one third the time it takes to read it regular. (*retreat - seminar - self-study - book*)

Genius Code

Tune into those secret messages that your brain automatically sends you to boost your IQ, solve any problem, accelerate learning, recognize golden opportunities, and supercharge your intuition. Take a fascinating exploration into the human mind with useful and practical applications that can benefit you immediately. (*self-study*)

Effortless Success

We create our lives, with every thought every minute of every day. The keys are to ask, believe, and receive. Best-selling author and transformational leader Jack Canfield translates these general principles into specific daily practices to help you create the life you want now. (*self-study*)

Spring Forest Qigong

An ancient Chinese "practice" called Qigong can take away stress, pain, and sickness at speeds that will amaze anyone...leaving you with more energy. You have seen people on television who could heal others with their touch. Or, who could pass healing energy to others. Now you can make use of this healing energy personally. *(retreat - seminar - self-study)*

Your Healing Power

This DVD follows a 6-day retreat led by teacher and healer Chunyi Lin and organized by Learning Strategies. In *Your Healing Power*, you'll see practitioners use Spring Forest Qigong, hear their commentary and personal insights, and witness miraculous healings. You will learn a soothing chant that helps heal the body, an easy way to reap healthful benefits of fasting, Chunyi Lin's process for helping another person heal, a powerful group healing method that you can use at home, and a sample exercise to experience the healing benefits of Spring Forest Qigong. *(DVD)*

Paraliminal Learning Sessions

Paraliminal audio programs help you maximize your potential by making changes and adjustments in your life. *(CDs)*

- Acquire new behaviors that help you reach goals and neutralize those that don't with the *New Behavior Generator.*
- Build confidence and immediately feel better about yourself with the *Self-Esteem Supercharger.*
- Gain freedom from fear with *Anxiety-Free.*
- Enter the deepest state of relaxation with *Deep Relaxation.*
- Turn on personal magnetism for poise, charm, and sex appeal with *Instantaneous Personal Magnetism.*
- Become youthful with unbridled vitality with *Youthful Vitality.*
- Reach and maintain your ideal weight without fad diets with *Ideal Weight.*
- Align your mind and body with *Perfect Health.*
- Eliminate procrastination and be effortlessly driven to achieve with *Get Around To It.*
- Eliminate negative self-talk and vaporize self-sabotage with *Automatic Pilot.*
- Strengthen belief in your ability to perform with *Belief.*

- Energize and become mentally alert with *10-Minute Supercharger*.
- Improve your memory instantly with *Memory Supercharger*.
- Use your true, natural genius for learning with *Personal Genius*.
- Feel love, peace, and joy toward yourself and the world around you with *Holiday Cheer*.
- Attract and/or improve relationships with *Positive Relationships*.
- Draw abundance into any area of your life with *Prosperity*.
- Remember and use your dreams for greater success in life with *Dream Play*.
- Change emotions and memories that stop you with *New History Generator*.
- Create new solutions and choices with *New Option Generator*.
- Develop the mental attitude and technical skills of a super salesperson with *Sales Leap*.
- Effortlessly cut back or give up smoking with *Smoke-Free*.
- Free yourself from addictive behaviors with *Break the Habit*.
- Ignite fun, attraction, and romance with *Creating Sparks*.
- Fire up your motivation for superior results with *Peak Performance*.
- Communicate with ease and project strength with *Talking to Win*.
- Make each moment a new beginning with *Fresh Start*.
- Think clearer, smarter, and faster with *Power Thinking*.
- Uncomplicate your life for more freedom and joy with *Simplicity*.
- Create a life that matters with *Success Built to Last*.
- Accomplish more in less time with *Focus & Concentration*.
- Build an unshakable inner home for happiness with *Happy for No Reason*.
- Consistently attract the good, positive, and extraordinary with *Living the Law of Attraction*.
- Gratefully receive life's abundant gifts with *You Deserve It!*

Memory Optimizer

Improve your memory with a unique, new approach using "The Bikenbihl Method" and "Paraliminal Learning." Concepts such as Intelligent Gap Management, the Inner Archive, Memory Pyramid, and the Anchorman List coupled with 57 memory tricks will give strength to your memory and ability to learn. *(self-study)*

Million Dollar Vocabulary

Sharpen your verbal edge for success. From the very first listening session your vocabulary will grow. Contains breakthrough processes to make it easier to learn over 600 words and their meanings so that you can use them effortlessly and naturally in everyday life. *(self-study)*

Resiliency

Use resiliency strategies to overcome adversity and thrive in most circumstances. Get both the edge to handle life's annoyances and setbacks as well as confidence to deal powerfully with cataclysmic events. Build mental and emotional flexibility to turn misfortune into good fortune. *(self-study)*

Abundance For Life

Most of us live in a trance, the illusion of limitation. Paul Scheele will take you on a journey from your familiar world to follow your hopes and dreams. You will free up energy as you awaken anew into a world of abundance, power and possibility. *(self-study)*

Genius Mind

Forget boring talks about "brain power"...this is a rock concert of mental potential. You'll see how the brain works and learn how to use this knowledge to further your financial, relationship, and academic success. *(DVD)*

Seeds of Enlightenment & Embracing Freedom

Jeddah Mali directs you to understand and interact with universal energy by leading you through a series of experiential explorations through your being. During these explorations you will find all of the grace of your being waiting patiently to be discovered. It is the being that *you have been all along. (self-study)*

Clear Mind ~ Bright Future

Bring your hopes and dreams into reality with this CD-ROM program. In just a couple of hours, international learning expert Paul Scheele will help you discover your guiding purpose in life, sort out what you really want, create a workable path, and get you on your way to manifesting your hopes and dreams. *(self-study)*

Sonic Access & Sonic Access Four Seasons

Align your body's energy system and quickly create significant and lasting change in virtually every area of your life with this extraordinary program. *Sonic Access* brings together Paul Scheele's unique Paraliminal technology, the audio frequencies of Holosync, the energy principles of Diamond Feng Shui, and the healing sounds of Spring Forest Qigong, all with the most transformative music you will ever experience. *Sonic Access Four Seasons* draws on the benevolent energies of nature to free your infinite spirit to excel and prosper. *(self-study)*

Diamond Feng Shui

Discover the enlightening world of Diamond Feng Shui, a revolutionary, yet straightforward, system to attract positive energy and deflect negative energy in your life. For thousands of years, Chinese emperors had access to sacred knowledge about how surroundings affect energy—for better and for worse. They called this knowledge Feng Shui, which means "wind" and "water." In this accessible and powerful course, you'll learn step by step how to change the energy of your home or workplace for immediate, long-lasting results in the four main areas of your life: success, relationships, health, and spiritual growth. *(self-study)*

Diamond Dowsing

Experience the ancient secrets of energy dowsing to control the energy around you. Marie Diamond teaches you step by step how to use dowsing rods, interpret their movements, and take appropriate action so you can neutralize stressed energy and amplify positive energy for your greater success, health, and well-being. *(self-study)*

How to Order or Enroll

You may order or enroll through the telephone, fax, mail, email, our secure website, or visiting us in person. If you do not already have a catalog and order form or enrollment materials, please contact us. Tell us which programs interest you so that we can best serve you.

All purchases come with a 30-day satisfaction guarantee, and you will be able to call specially trained coaches for assistance.

We are pleased to serve you.